UNCOMMON PAPER FLOWERS

UNCOMMON

Extraordinary Botanicals and
How to Craft Them

PAPER

KATE ALARCÓN

Still-life photography by Alice Gao

CHRONICLE BOOKS
SAN FRANCISCO

FLOWERS

Library of Congress Cataloging-in-Publication Data available.

ISBN 978-1-4521-7693-2

Manufactured in China.

Photography (Part I) by ALICE GAO.
Prop styling (Part I) by KIRA CORBIN.
Photography (Part II) by LIZ DALY.
Design by LIZZIE VAUGHAN.
Typesetting by JARED GENTZ.
Typeset in GOTHAM, GRENALE, AND CASLON.

10 9 8 7 6 5 4 3 2 1

CHRONICLE BOOKS LLC
680 Second Street
San Francisco, CA 94107
www.chroniclebooks.com

THE FOLLOWING TRADEMARKS WERE USED IN THIS BOOK:
Aleene's Original Tacky Glue is a registered trademark of Duncan
Enterprises DBA iLoveToCreate Corporation; Art-C is a registered
trademark of Momenta, Inc.; BazzillBasicsPaper is a registered
trademark of Bazzill Basics Paper, Inc.; BBC is a registered
trademark of The British Broadcasting Corporation; Canson
Mi-Teintes is a registered trademark of Canson Societe Par Actions
Simplifee; Colortool is a registered trademark of Design Master
Color Tool, Inc.; Copic is a registered trademark of Kabushiki Kaisha
Too (Too Corporation) Corporation; Core'dinations is a registered
trademark of American Crafts, L.C.; Darice cardstock is a registered
trademark of Darice, Inc.; DecoArt is a registered trademark of
DecoArt, Inc.; Design Master is a registered trademark of Design
Master Color Tool, Inc.; Elmer's is a registered trademark of Sanford,
L.P.; Faber-Castell PITT Artist Pen is a registered trademark of
Faber-Castell Aktiengesellschaft Corporation; FolkArt Home Decor
is a registered trademark of Plaid Enterprises, Inc.; Krylon is a
registered trademark of SWIMC LLC; Mod Podge is a registered
trademark of Plaid Enterprises, Inc.; Nuvo is a registered trademark
of Tonic Studios Limited; PanPastel is a registered trademark
of Bernadette Ward and Ladd Forsline; Pringles is a registered
trademark of Pringles LLC; Prismacolor Premier is a registered
trademark of Sanford, L.P. Newell Operating Company; TintIT. is a
registered trademark of Design Master Color Tool, Inc.; Tsukineko is
a registered trademark of Tsukineko Co., Ltd.; Werola is a registered
trademark of Seaman Paper Asia Company Ltd.

Contents

PART I

The Flora
13

Uncommon Plant Kingdom

The plant kingdom—with its spines, spikes, tendrils, crinkles, tufts, trumpets, purses, and pistils—is both spectacularly diverse and deeply strange. It offers the paper flower maker an inexhaustible variety of forms, textures, and colors to attempt to re-create. The plants and flowers that seduce me into devoting hours (and sometimes even weeks) to re-creating them are often the dark and the unusual, the overlooked and the underused. I love to try to capture the creepy beauty of a carnivorous plant or the fairy-tale quality of a foxglove.

The flora you'll find here are uncommon in a few different ways: some are oddly shaped and little known, like the star cactus (*Astrophytum asterias*) or jack-in-the-pulpit. Some, like the spider plant and red hot poker, are familiar enough in the garden or greenhouse but not often used in arrangements. Some are lesser-known varieties of cut flower favorites like roses, peonies, and poppies.

The plants and flowers in these pages are organized by habitat. I chose flowers for each environment with a clear picture of the habitat in mind—a clearing at the edge of a forest, a desert in bloom, a slightly unruly cutting garden. Grouped by landscape, the plants and flowers in each section seem at home together and reveal shapes and textures that they have in common—the delicate forms of the woodland plants and the sculptural qualities of cacti, for example. But I also love to mix flowers from different environments to create playful, unexpected arrangements. As you craft your own paper flowers, I hope you'll feel free to pair anthuriums with succulents, or opium poppies with cobra lilies. Part of the fun of making uncommon flowers is using them in uncommon arrangements.

Translating Nature in Paper

Paper flower making might seem like a fairly narrow pursuit: it's a craft that basically requires you to translate one subject (flora) into one medium (paper). But the almost infinite variety found within the plant kingdom, the wide array of paper stocks, and a whole universe of surface design techniques provide tremendous room for the paper flower artist to experiment and innovate. It's an ever-evolving craft teeming with fresh challenges and puzzles to solve: making a lichen is vastly different from making a poppy, and being an expert at rose-making isn't much help when you're trying to craft mushrooms.

Although paper flower making requires a measure of artistic flair to achieve a convincing lifelike appearance, you must first understand the basic construction of a given plant or flower type, especially for more complex and unusual designs. Because I'm drawn to such a broad range of plant life, I spend a lot of time developing the technical ability to make a new plant or flower. For some designs, in order to make a particular flower or plant I'll refer back to a series of successful techniques developed through trial and error in earlier projects. That aspect of the design process—the unlocking of one technique that opens up the possibility of another project, with its own puzzles—is a central part of what I find compelling about paper flowers. A lot of what you'll see in the following pages is a result of restlessness and curiosity.

When I begin a new paper flower project, usually I'll start by identifying the elements I feel uncertain about—maybe it's the fuzzy center of a king protea or the gills of a mushroom—and tackle those first. Working out these elements first ensures that I don't end up with a flower that's perfect except that it completely lacks an essential element, like the center or gills. Then, once I've figured out all the elements—center, petal shape, leaves, colors—I'll start putting the plant together. Often, especially if it's a very involved plant, I'll make half of one, just to make sure I have my model right. Once I'm pretty confident in the design, I start putting the full structure together. Usually if I'm making multiples of something, I'm tweaking the design with each additional flower. I find the hard deadline of a class or tutorial helpful, since it forces me to commit to a finished design and write the instructions for a project that might still feel imperfect to me. Every few weeks I sweep my workspace for projects that are half worked up and not going anywhere, and I dump them into a big plastic box that I keep in my craft closet.

Over the years the box has become a big, messy reference space full of potentially cool ideas, dead ends, and half-solved puzzles.

As much as I love to solve a botanical puzzle now, I was completely consumed when I first got started. Above all, I wanted my work to be mistakable for the real thing, and I needed to figure out a lot of techniques to achieve that goal. I threw myself into trial and error and experimentation, and I thrilled at each problem solved. But the more realistic my work became, the less satisfied I was with the goal of realism. I began to appreciate the artistry that emerged from the gaps between a flower as it was in nature and the flower I could make.

The unique style I've developed is usually most evident when I'm being resourceful—improvising to make a design happen even if it's not an exact copy. Now I try to be thoughtful about how realistic and how stylized I'd like a design to be. I like the playfulness of a mix of levels of realism. My Echeveria succulents (page 127), one of the first designs I felt really proud of, are a good example of finding a balance between a plant that looks real and one that looks constructed, though I didn't quite appreciate it when I first made them. Each leaf is carefully painted and embossed to look just like a real echeveria from the top, but when viewed from the side, the backs of the leaves give it all away, revealing that the fleshy leaves are actually just bent paper. And since there's no coloring on the back of the leaves, you can see the jewel tones of the unpainted paper. With the side exposed, you can see the realism and fakery at once. The bright color on the unpainted side bounces off the powdery, plain, purplish surface of the tops of the petals, creating a subtle glow. Part of the beauty of paper flowers is the painted and unpainted elements working together, complementing one another.

Finding Inspiration

Nothing will make you notice plant life like trying to re-create it. And once you begin paper flower crafting, you'll start to notice botanical inspiration everywhere. The retail plaza where I do most of my shopping has glazed planters filled with beautiful flowers, which are replenished with new varieties every season. Whenever I see the planters, I consider surreptitiously swiping a flower to serve as inspiration for a paper design. (My occasional floral theft—just a single flower head, just one little leaf!—distresses my exceptionally upstanding children. I mostly defer to them; after all, someday they may be the ones bailing me out after someone catches me making off with a pansy head. In my mug shot, I'll have dirt on my face and leaves in my hair.) And though I would never dream of pilfering blooms from the beautiful home gardens I pass every day while walking my dog, I'll admit that I sometimes very casually collect a few fallen petals to trace at home. Even bits and pieces of a plant can be of enormous help in refining the design of a paper bloom.

Paper flower making might set your mind working feverishly to solve every plant you encounter outside—botanical gardens should come with a warning label for this reason. But the true bliss of making paper flowers is going outside and marveling at what you'll never perfectly capture, either because a plant is too complex or because there's just too much of it to try to re-create. When I surrender to that impossibility, I'm in awe of the plant kingdom.

HOW TO USE THIS BOOK

The following pages are organized into three sections. Whether you're a flower enthusiast, a nature lover, a paper flower maker, or a general crafter, I hope you'll find beauty and adventure ahead.

PART I

The Flora presents portraits of thirty plants organized by natural environment. Each portrait is presented alongside information about the floral's history, folklore, and meaning. (The meaning of a flower was often derived from the language of flowers, an ancient, elaborate code used in the Middle East, Asia, and Europe. It was said that this code allowed lovers to secretly exchange messages through small bouquets of flowers that conveyed specific sentiments.)

PART II

In Foundational Tools and Techniques, you'll find detailed information on the tools and materials you'll need and instructions for the essential techniques in paper flower making. This section is essential for readers making the projects in this book and will also be of interest to noncrafters seeking a behind-the-scenes look into paper flower making.

PART III

Making the Flowers presents the detailed step-by-step instructions for making the projects in Part I using techniques from Part II.

PART I

The Flora

Woodland

Foxglove

COMMON NAMES: fairy caps, fairy thimbles, fairy gloves, witch's gloves, dead man's bells, throatwort, witch's thimbles

LATIN NAME: *Digitalis purpurea*

MEANING: insincerity, a wish

SEE PAGE 103

Though the name "foxglove" might conjure an image of refined foxes prancing on their hind legs, a little glove on each paw, many insist that the name is a corruption of "folk's gloves," or rather, fairy folk's gloves. But it turns out that this etymology is far from settled. The Old English from which we get the name has no tradition of fairies, and the simplest explanation for the "fox" in foxglove is that it corresponds with the Old English word for fox. Oxford etymologist Anatoly Liberman declares with finality: "In sum, *foxglove* means *foxglove*, and this disturbing fact has to be accepted." May the fancy foxes prance in celebration!

The magic of the foxglove lies not in its association with the world of fairies but in its medicinal properties. Digitalis has been used to treat cardiac ailments since the eighteenth century and continues to be prescribed today. One of the possible side effects of taking digitalis is a color vision deficiency called xanthopsia, which causes the eyes to see the world through a yellow filter, exaggerating yellows at the expense of other colors. Medical historiographers have speculated that Vincent van Gogh's striking yellows may have been a result of digitalis-induced xanthopsia. Digitalis was widely prescribed in the nineteenth century for ailments ranging from stomach complaints to mental illness, and van Gogh may have begun taking the drug during his stay in Saint-Paul Asylum in 1889. Proponents of this theory point to a portrait van Gogh painted of his doctor, Dr. Paul-Ferdinand Gachet, holding a foxglove stem as evidence.

In fact, van Gogh favored yellows even before his treatment at the asylum, and his vision was tested while taking the drug and found to be excellent. Further, scholars doubt whether he would have survived doses of digitalis sufficient to experience prolonged xanthopsia. Like the old stories about foxgloves and fairy folk, the tale of van Gogh's foxglove vision is likely as apocryphal as it is enchanting.

Jack-in-the-Pulpit

COMMON NAMES: Preacher John, brown dragon,

devil's dear, wake robin

LATIN NAME: *Arisaema triphyllum*

MEANING: passion

SEE PAGE 106

Jack-in-the-pulpit is an odd little wildflower, native to North America. The spadix, a blunt spike in the flower's center, evokes a preacher (Jack) ensconced in his pulpit, a leaflike structure called a spathe. The bottom half of the spathe forms a tube around the bottom of the spadix and the tiny flowers that grow there. The top half of the spathe forms an overhang that prevents the tube from filling with rainwater. Though this little funnel traps insects, jack-in-the-pulpits are not actually carnivorous plants—the trapped insects are pollinators, not prey.

The male jack—so called because it produces tiny male flowers—holds its pollen at the bottom of the spadix, inside the tube formed by the spathe, which means that it can't spread its pollen through the air. Instead, jack-in-the-pulpits attract pollinating insects by emitting an odor that has been compared to stagnant water and fungi. When a gnat climbs down the spathe in pursuit of the odor's source, it soon finds that the tube is too slippery to crawl back up. Its fate now depends on the sex of the plant. Male pollinators have a little opening at the bottom of the spathe that allows the pollen-covered gnat to escape. If all goes according to plan for the plant, the gnat will then crawl into the tube of a female flower (or jill, as it is sometimes playfully called). Unlike the jack, the jill has no escape hatch, which ensures maximum pollination.

This faux-carnivorous system isn't the plant's only clever adaptation. Jack-in-the-pulpits have evolved another strategy for adapting to difficult conditions, called sequential hermaphroditism. When resources are scarce, a plant that produced only female flowers can switch sexes, producing male flowers, which don't need as much energy because they don't need to do the heavy lifting of reproduction: storing enough energy to produce berries. When conditions improve, the plant can switch back to producing female flowers.

Log with Moss & Lichen

COMMON NAME: moss	COMMON NAME: lichen	SEE PAGE 111
LATIN NAME: Bryophytae	MEANING: melancholy	
MEANING: maternal love		

Amid the beautiful, delicate, and varied woodland flowers and plants, it's easy to overlook a botanical feature like a fallen log. Yet these features teem with life and perform a number of vital services for a forest ecosystem. Downed logs play an essential role in the health of a forest, hosting decomposers who help return organic matter to the soil, preventing erosion and moisture loss, and increasing biodiversity by providing habitat and nourishment for a wide variety of flora and fauna.

As a fallen log begins to break down, its bark becomes loose, granting easy access to insects, which in turn create a feast for birds. Over time the center of the log grows soft, which allows small mammals like chipmunks to burrow through, providing cover from predators. Eventually, the core becomes hollow, and a fox or coyote might claim the space as a den. And airborne seeds that settle on the log may sprout, producing new saplings rising from old wood.

Mosses and lichens aid the process of decay by retaining moisture and preventing water from evaporating on the log's surface. Though these ancient and primitive growths often appear together and can share similarities of form, mosses and lichens are not related.

While moss is a plant, lichen is a symbiotic organism, a partnership between multiple fungi and algae. The filaments of the fungi provide a structure that surrounds the algae, which do the work of photosynthesis, allowing the lichen to turn sunlight into energy. Although lichen and moss are often confused, the language of flowers assigns them very different meanings: moss signifies maternal love, while lichen expresses solitude and dejection.

Rosy Bonnet

LATIN NAME: *Mycena rosea*

MEANING: suspicion

SEE PAGE 114

This beautiful pink mushroom grows in clusters near the base of trees. In its early stages of growth, a new bonnet has the classic convex, rounded cap you might associate with mushrooms. As the mushroom matures, the cap flattens and becomes concave around the edges, exposing the row of gills underneath. This slightly inverted cap isn't a perfect circle, but rather an irregular disk that gives the mushroom a whimsical, fairy-tale quality. The caps can range from very pale to deep pink, with the color most concentrated at the cap's center and fading at its edges.

The rosy bonnet contains potentially lethal amounts of muscarine, a toxic alkaloid that when ingested acts on the central nervous system, causing airway paralysis, intestinal spasms, pulmonary edema, and even death. Muscarine poisoning usually occurs when a forager mistakes a poisonous mushroom for an edible one. As the language of flowers suggests, it's safest to regard wild mushrooms with extreme suspicion and obtain an expert opinion before eating.

Bleeding Mycena

SEE PAGE 119

COMMON NAMES: blood-foot mushroom, bleeding fairy helmet, burgundydrop bonnet, bleeding bellcap

LATIN NAME: *Mycena haemotopus*

MEANING: suspicion

The bleeding mycena (pronounced "my-SEEN-uh") grows in clusters on decaying wood and on diseased areas of living trees, sometimes sprouting from the cracks in dead logs. Its bell-shaped caps come in a range of brownish pinks, with pale gills underneath. For such a lovely little mushroom, it has a range of sinister common names, including the tragic-sounding "bleeding fairy helmet." Even its Latin species name, *haemotopus*, comes from the Greek *haemato*, or blood and pus or foot. A curious trait inspired these grim monikers: when you cut the stipe (or stem) of these diminutive fungi, a dark red liquid drips from the site of the injury. This bloody excretion is actually latex, which is thought to protect the mushroom by gumming up the mouths of insect predators.

The drama of these little mushrooms doesn't stop there: bleeding mycena are also bioluminescent, emitting a faint but steady greenish glow. This glow, sometimes called foxfire or fairy fire (the same bioluminescence found in fireflies and angler fish), results from a chemical reaction between the compound luciferin and the enzyme luciferase, which release light energy when combined. Scientists theorize that the fungi's glow is a reproductive strategy to draw spore-spreading insects. Surprisingly, the mushrooms seem to know when to deploy this secret weapon: they don't waste their fairy fire during the day, when daylight would make it invisible. Instead, bioluminescent fungi light up only at night, when their glow will show to best effect.

These crafted mushrooms, presented with stipes sliced and bleeding, make for a striking table display. Unfortunately, real bleeding mycena haven't been tested for enough types of toxicity to make them safe to eat.

Calypso Orchid

COMMON NAMES: Venus's slipper orchid, lady

slipper orchid, fairy slipper orchid, deer's head orchid

LATIN NAME: *Calypso bulbosa*

SEE PAGE 122

This spectacular woodland orchid's name evokes Calypso, the beautiful nymph who enchanted Homer's Odysseus, holding him prisoner on her island until Zeus ordered his release. In fact, like the nymph, the orchid's name derives from the Greek word for "hidden," since the plant grows tucked away in sheltered areas on the forest floor.

Besides being one of the more beautiful woodland orchids, and the only species in its whole genus, the calypso is of special interest to botanists because of its reproduction strategy. A yellow beard of tiny, pollen-bearing hairs sits at the entrance to a little purse, or slipper. Toward the back of this purse are nectaries, organs that secrete nectar. Lured by a sweet vanilla-like odor, an insect visits the purse only to find that it has been duped—the nectary is a fake, and there's nothing to eat. Covered in pollen, the disappointed insect moves on, pollinating the next calypso that draws it in. This strategy, called food deception, has the added benefit of helping the plant avoid inbreeding. Eventually, the insect will abandon that patch of calypso, looking farther away for food. When it encounters another calypso it may not recognize it: small variations in color and form can deceive the insect into repeating its mistake, this time pollinating a more distantly related bloom.

Newly emerged queen bumblebees are one of the calypso's most important pollinators (worker bees are too large to fit into its dainty purse.) Like the jack-in-the-pulpit, this orchid is not carnivorous but is still quite unkind to insect visitors (though the calypso doesn't have an assigned meaning in the language of flowers, "false promise" might be fitting).

Desert

Echeveria

COMMON NAMES: hen and chicks, Mexican snowball, Mexican gem

LATIN NAME: *Echeveria*

SEE PAGE 127

These charming succulents, made up of rosettes of fleshy leaves in subtle, watercolor tones, are long-lived and fairly easy to care for. The leaves have a powdery, sea-glass quality called the bloom, or, less romantically, epicuticular wax. This wax, which also appears on the surface of plums and blueberries, acts as sunblock, protecting the echeveria from UV rays. It also prevents moisture loss and water damage: the whitish film allows the plant to repel water, which is why water droplets bead up on succulent leaves.

Though the echeveria's rosette of leaves may make it look like a flower, the plant's flowers are actually arching spikes of tiny flowers in orange, yellow, or white, which are pollinated by bees and hummingbirds.

The language of flowers has little to say about the succulent, but with its numerous methods of sexual and asexual reproduction, "fertility" might be considered as a possible meaning for the plant. One of its common names, hen and chicks, refers to the mini-echeveria offsets that cluster around a mature plant. Tiny echeveria will also grow on the base of a leaf plucked from the succulent, and a beheaded mother plant will grow pups on its stump.

Echeveria, which comes in an array of complex pinks, purples, greens, and oranges, is fittingly named for a watercolorist, Atanasio Echeverría y Godoy. Echeverría y Godoy, a nineteenth-century Mexican botanical artist and explorer, was part of "Flora Méxicana," an ambitious expedition to document the flora and fauna of Mexico. His field studies captured the color and form of collected plant specimens while they still retained their shape and color. Because of political instability, the "Flora Méxicana" project was never completed; fortunately, Echeverría y Godoy's masterful illustrations survived.

DESERT

Blue Torch Cactus

COMMON NAMES: tree cactus, blue candle

SEE PAGE 130

LATIN NAME: *Pilosocereus azureus*

MEANING: endurance

The blue torch is a columnar cactus that can grow to be 12 ft (3.7 m) tall when cultivated, and up to 30 ft (9 m) tall in the wild. This impressive succulent is native to arid regions of Brazil, where it grows in both rocky and sandy terrain. Its Latin genus name means "hairy cereus," as most pilosocereus cacti have both spines and wisps of white fibers growing together out of the areoles that run up and down the cactus. In some pilosocereuses, like the old man cactus, the white fibers are so long and thick that they seem to form a cloud around the plant. The hair on a blue torch, though, is much more subtle.

The blue torch's skin varies from sea green to robin's egg blue and even turquoise. The intensity of the blue color can vary even for a single plant. A young blue torch will become more intensely blue when it grows to maturity. A mature plant may sport even richer blues if moved to a sunnier location. The plant's color comes from a wax that protects the cactus from the sun; when stripped of the wax, the plant's skin is a much less distinctive green.

The cactus has charms beyond its blue coloring, including rows of golden spines that run up and down its ribs. Interlaced with these spines are the classic fine strands of fibers. The plant's large, white, funnel-shaped flowers bloom at night, attracting pollinators like bats and sphinx moths.

If you see a real blue torch cactus, don't touch it. While you may have the dexterity to avoid the golden spines, your touch might disturb the wax that makes the cactus's skin blue and protects it from the sun. You definitely don't want your fingerprints all over someone's prized blue cactus.

Prickly Pear Cactus

COMMON NAMES: barbary pear, cactus pear,

Indian fig, tuna fig

LATIN NAME: *Opuntia*

MEANING: satire

SEE PAGE 135

A prickly pear cactus is made up of flat, fleshy pads, protected by a wicked combination of spines and glochids, barbed hairs that lodge in a predator's skin. The pads bear dark red fruit, rich in fiber and antioxidants. Native to the Americas, the prickly pear has long been used by indigenous people as a source of nutrition, hydration, and medicine. In Mexican cuisine, both the fruits, or tunas, and the pads, or nopales, are carefully stripped and used to make a variety of both savory and sweet dishes.

This cactus plays an important role in the story of the founding of Tenochtitlan, the capital of the ancient Aztec empire. As the story goes, the Aztecs had recently migrated from the north and settled in the Valley of Mexico in the city of Culhuacan. Having helped the king of Culhuacan win an important battle, the Aztecs were rewarded with the gift of the king's daughter, whom the Aztecs were expected to worship as a goddess.

When the king came to visit his daughter, he found one of the Aztecs wearing her skin. The Aztec explained that Huitzilpochtli (pronounced "weet-sil-POACHED-li"), the Aztec god of the sun, war, and human sacrifice, had demanded that the king's

daughter be sacrificed to him. A battle ensued, and the Aztecs lost. Exiled, they were left to wander in search of a new homeland, carrying a large stone statue of Huitzilpochtli in hopes of winning his assistance.

Meanwhile, Huitzilpochtli had become angry with his nephew, Copil, who had betrayed him. In his wrath, Huitzilpochtli cut out his nephew's heart and threw it as far as he could. It landed on an island (now, Mexico City) in the middle of a lake. From the heart grew a prickly pear cactus, studded with fruits that resemble human hearts. Huitzilpochtli told the Aztec priests to look for an eagle perched atop a prickly pear cactus, eating a snake. The Aztecs found the island and, seeing this sign, established Tenochtitlan. The modern-day coat of arms of Mexico features the bird, snake, and prickly pear cactus.

Night-Blooming Cereus

COMMON NAMES: queen of the night,

Dutchman's pipe cactus, orchid cactus

LATIN NAME: *Epiphyllum oxypetalum*

MEANING: transient beauty

SEE PAGE 138

"We'd sit mesmerized, as the bud trembled and shuddered while it unwound its long slender white petals and spread them before our incredulous eyes as a delicately incised saucer full of froth," wrote poet Hubert Creekmore, a member of Eudora Welty's Cereus Society. The "society," composed of Welty's artistic and literary friends, would gather on her porch to celebrate the one night of the year the flowers on her night-blooming cereus would open and, only hours later, wither.

Cereus fans and botanical gardens celebrate this strange floral event, but the logistics of planning a blooming party can be difficult, since it's hard to predict exactly which day the flower will bloom. Temperature, moisture, and even the phases of the moon seem to affect the timing. Cereus plants growing near each other will often bloom on the same night, leading scientists to hypothesize that the plants use some form of chemical communication to time the bloom, ensuring that flowers on multiple plants are available for pollination.

Because they open at night, when bees and butterflies are scarce, night-blooming cacti depend on nocturnal pollinators like bats and moths, which are attracted to the flower's heavy magnolia scent and white petals that seem to glow in the moonlight. Some bats hover over the bloom and daintily sip nectar by means of a very long tongue, while others just perch on the flower and stick their whole head in.

Much of the night-blooming cereus's symbolism derives from the ephemeral nature of the flowers. To the Victorians, the flower represented fleeting beauty; in China, such flowers represent short-lived glory. In India, a similar night-blooming flower is called *Brahma Kamal*. It's said that Brahma, the Hindu god of creation, lives in the flower, and if a supplicant prays during the brief time the bloom is open, the prayer will be answered.

Welty's Cereus Society's motto had a more lighthearted take on the strange flower: "Don't take it 'cereus,' life's too mysterious."

Agave

COMMON NAMES: century plant, maguey,

American aloe, Mexican aloe

LATIN NAME: *Agave*

MEANING: bitterness

SEE PAGE 143

Although they are often mistaken for cacti, agaves are actually succulents. Native to the American Southwest and Mexico, agave has been an essential food source for indigenous peoples for thousands of years. The leaves, flowers, stalk, and heart of the agave are all edible, and its juice can be fermented to produce alcoholic beverages like pulque, mezcal, and tequila.

Tequila is made from blue agave, which takes six to eight years to mature and develop the right amount of fructose. When the plant is ready for harvest, all its leaves are removed by a *jimedor*, an expert agave farmer, and its huge heart is exposed. The heart, which can weigh up to 240 lb (109 kg), is then baked and mashed to extract the juice, which is fermented and distilled to make tequila.

This sculptural plant forms a rosette of smooth, sword-shaped leaves. Early in the plant's life the leaves are packed tightly at the center of the rosette, the spines of the leaves pressed against each other. As the rosette grows and unfolds, the agave leaves bear an impression of the spines of their rosette-mates.

It can take an agave up to forty years to store enough energy to flower, but the truly impressive flower stalk is well worth the wait. An agave flower stalk can grow up to 30 ft (9 m) tall and bears small tubular flowers that attract Mexican long-nosed bats. These bats reach the flower's nectar by inserting their long muzzles into the tubular flowers.

Sadly, the flower marks the end of the agave's life cycle. After the agave blooms, it dies, in a reproductive strategy known as semelparity. The agave expends all of its resources on a single fatal reproductive event, reserving no additional energy to sustain itself afterward. The dead agave leaves behind several pups, or little agave offsets, to take its place.

Star Cactus

COMMON NAMES: sand dollar cactus, sea urchin

cactus, star peyote

LATIN NAME: *Astrophytum asterias*

SEE PAGE 146

This little cactus looks a bit like a tiny green pumpkin that's sprouted a set of tassels and a crown of flowers. Its genus name, *Astrophytum*, means "star plant" and refers to the way that, when viewed from above, lines of wooly tufts appear to radiate out from its center. Star cacti grow in scrubby areas of southern Texas and northeastern Mexico. Small and squat, they're easy to miss when they're nestled into the gravel. But when the cacti burst into bloom in late spring, their flowers dazzle.

The star cactus's body is made up of between five and eleven ribs, each dotted down the middle with tufts of woolly fibers. The cactus is completely spineless, but the tufts of hair might give you pause, since they so closely resemble glochids, the devilish little fibers that embed themselves in the skin of anyone inexperienced enough to touch them. But the fur on a star cactus is completely benign. It grows from structures called areoles, which in other cacti may produce spines, glochids, flowers, and branches. In fact, it's the presence of areoles that distinguishes cacti from other succulents.

Star cacti are endangered in the wild, where they continue to be illegally collected. Fortunately, cultivated star cacti are available through the nursery trade: they make interesting, sculptural houseplants and have been grown indoors since the mid-nineteenth century. Just be sure to water with a light hand, because overwatering star cacti can be disastrous. Because the bottom half is sunk in the soil, it's easy for the underside to rot if kept too wet. Even more alarming is the fact that a star cactus that has absorbed too much water can swell and actually crack its hard outer shell. But a star cactus in bloom is pure delight and a gardening accomplishment to be proud of, so the little extra care that can persuade yours to flower is more than worth it.

Glasshouse

Anthurium

COMMON NAMES: tail flower, flamingo flower,

laceleaf, painted tongue, boy flower

LATIN NAME: *Anthurium andraeanum*

MEANING: hospitality

SEE PAGE 151

Native to tropical regions of Central and South America, most anthuriums are epiphytes, organisms that grow on the surface of another plant. Anthuriums, which grow on moss and fallen leaves caught between branches, get their name from the Greek word *anthos*, meaning "flower," and *oura*, meaning "tail." In fact, "tail flower" is one of this plant's common names.

What might look like a flower—the colorful, heart-shaped "petal" with a spike for a center—is actually an inflorescence, a cluster of flowers growing on a single stem. In this case, tiny flowers grow up and down the spadix—the tapered rod in the center of the inflorescence. The single shiny "petal" is a spathe, a modified leaf that protects the spadix while it matures.

The spadix contains both male and female flowers, making the inflorescence bisexual (also called "perfect" in plant speak). It has both male and female reproductive structures; thus, an anthurium could potentially pollinate itself, leading to a loss of genetic diversity. The plant solves this problem by having the female and male flowers take turns. First the female flowers become receptive to pollination; when that phase is finished, the male flowers release their pollen. When an insect visits a male flower and picks up his pollen, it will skip over the spent female flowers on this particular spadix and fly off to a spadix on another anthurium plant, where ideally it will deposit the pollen on a receptive female flower.

Known for their undemanding nature and their extremely long-lived blooms, anthuriums may seem a little bit commonplace and unglamorous. But they make lovely cut flowers, and fashionable florists often include anthuriums in compositions alongside more traditional cut flowers for a stunning effect.

Spider Orchid

COMMON NAMES: cricket orchid

SEE PAGE 154

LATIN NAME: *Brassia caudata*

The spider orchid evokes its arachnid namesake in several ways. The lip, or labellum, is the apron-like petal that grows from the bottom of the center of the flower and its slight arch suggests a rounded spider's body. Five thin, elongated "petals," resembling legs, radiate from the body. The petals—actually three petals and two sepals—curve backward, further evoking a spider pose. The flowers hang suspended in the air on their arched stems like spiders in a web.

The spider orchid's blooms have actually evolved to mimic spiders. The arachnid-like flower lures the female spider-hunter wasp, also known, terrifyingly, as a tarantula hawk. The wasp attacks the faux "spider," repeatedly stinging it in the "abdomen"—that is, the orchid's lip—and seizing its "head," which is actually the column, a nub at the center of the flower. As the wasp struggles to subdue her prey, her head is covered in pollen. Eventually, when she gives up and continues on her hunt, she may mistake another brassia flower for a spider and, during her next attack, inadvertently fertilize it with the pollen she is carrying. Whether she ever realizes she has been deceived or assumes she has just tangled with some very tenacious spiders is a mystery.

The spider orchid is native to Mexico, Brazil, Bolivia, the Caribbean, and Florida, though it hasn't been seen in Florida since the 1990s and is believed to be extirpated there (extirpation has occurred when a plant species becomes extinct in one of its native habitats).

Blushing Bride Tillandsia

COMMON NAMES: sky plant, air plant

SEE PAGE 159

LATIN NAME: *Tillandsia ionantha*

Native to Central America and Mexico, tillandsias—also commonly known as air plants—are popular houseplants thanks to their ability to grow in or on just about any support system. Although these epiphytes grow on host trees and other plants, they aren't parasites; the host simply provides a physical support that allows them to grow up off the ground (inorganic supports like utility lines and fence posts can also act as support systems for tillandsias).

Although they produce small roots, these serve only to anchor them in place on host plants. Because they aren't parasites, tillandsias need to absorb their own water and food. Air plants absorb nutrients directly through their leaves via minute organs called trichomes, tiny hair-like scales that cover both sides of the leaf. Each trichome is composed of a nail-shaped shield of dead cells and a little stalk connecting the shield to the leaf. Moisture is wicked up by the dead cells and passes through the stalk into the leaf. This process, in which cells die in a fixed sequence as a normal part of the plant's development, is called apoptosis, or programmed cell death.

Trichomes not only give tillandsias their powdery appearance but also can provide helpful information about the air plant species' preferred environment. Plants with more powdery leaves usually favor more arid regions, where they need a heavy coating of trichomes for both hydration and sun protection. More lightly coated leaves indicate that the plant flourishes in a setting with less intense sunlight and more plentiful moisture.

Tillandsias can seem almost magical in their ability to survive completely unrooted in soil, but they actually do require care in watering. The popular advice to keep them misted can do the plant more harm than good. When the trichomes are constantly swollen with water, it is difficult for the plants to aspirate. A good soak every week or two, with intermittent spritzing now and then, will keep an air plant hydrated and breathing easy.

Lady's Slipper Orchid

COMMON NAMES: Venus slipper

LATIN NAME: *Paphiopedilum*

MEANING: capricious beauty

SEE PAGE 162

Paphiopedilums—or paphs, as they're often called by horticulturalists—are mostly terrestrial orchids native to Southeast Asia. Scientists believe these bizarre-looking plants may be among the oldest, most primitive orchid types growing today.

The genus name, which literally translates as "Aphrodite's sandal," refers to the orchid's pouch. This pouch, or saccate labellum, is a modified petal that attracts and captures insects. Lady's slippers may look and act like a carnivorous plant, but they trap insects only as a means of spreading pollen. The orchid attracts its pollinators, often flies or small bees, using scent. Lured by an odor that can range from floral to fetid, the insect lands on what appears to be a suitable perch in the center of the flower but is actually a slippery wart on an organ called a staminode. Unable to find its footing, the insect drops into the purse.

Once inside, the insect finds that the inner walls of the trap are far too slippery to climb. The only means of escape is a ladder of upward-growing hairs at the very back of the pouch. This ladder routes the insect directly to the stigma, the flower's female reproductive organ. If the insect has visited another lady's slipper earlier in the day, any pollen it is carrying will rub off onto the stigma. The insect has only to push past the anthers—the male organs—to escape, but in doing so, it picks up a fresh load of pollen to deposit on its next adventure.

Sustainably raised lady's slippers can be highly rewarding houseplants. Coax them into bloom, and the flowers will last up to three months. Because the orchids usually grow on forest floors, they don't require a lot of light; a spot in an east-facing window will likely please a paph. And since lady's slippers aren't actually carnivorous, they don't require insect meals—all they need is liquid fertilizer, which is much less of a chore to acquire.

Spider Plant

COMMON NAMES: airplane plant, St. Bernard's lily,

spider ivy, ribbon plant, hen and chickens

LATIN NAME: *Chlorophytum comosum*

SEE PAGE 167

The spider plant is the ultimate houseplant: it's easy to propagate and hard to kill, and it produces runners bearing miniature spider plants that cascade down from the mother plant.

Spider plants were brought to Europe from Africa as specimens to study and collect, and they were grown in glasshouses and conservatories by wealthy collectors. As glass became cheaper, houseplants became a more accessible luxury. By the Victorian era, houseplants were de rigueur for the respectable middle-class home, where they were displayed in baskets, elaborate planters, and glass Wardian cases, and atop pedestals and plant stands. The spider plant was the perfect plant to grow in the ornate hanging baskets so popular at the time.

After the Victorian houseplant vogue passed, houseplants came to be seen as fussy, impractical, and old-fashioned. It wasn't until the 1950s that Scandinavian influence on midcentury design brought houseplants back into favor. But this time, simple wooden planters were favored over fancy urns. By the 1970s, houseplants were everywhere, and potted spider plants were ideal occupants for the macramé hangers of that era.

What's uncommon about this ubiquitous plant is the incredible opportunity it affords to watch asexual reproduction unfold. The spider plant's plantlets—or spiderettes—share the exact genetics of the mother plant, making them clones. These baby plants quickly develop adventitious roots, which will take hold if the spiderette finds itself in contact with soil. They root easily in water and will eventually produce their own offsets, which will have a genetic makeup identical to their grandmother plant.

Long-Petaled Bulbophyllum

LATIN NAME: *Bulbophyllum longissimum*

SEE PAGE 170

Native to Thailand, Burma, Borneo, and Malaysia, long-petaled bulbophyllum is a member of the largest genus of the Orchidaceae family. This highly diverse genus contains more than two thousand species, including such highlights as *Bulbophyllum beccarii*, an orchid that smells like dead elephants; *Bulbophyllum medusa*, whose big tuft of a flower evokes a Dr. Seuss character; and the *phalaenopsis* that can be found at many grocery stores.

The long-petaled bulbophyllum is an arresting plant that produces arching spikes bearing extremely long, tubular flowers arranged in half circles. The trailing flowers narrow and become filiform—spindly and threadlike—toward the bottom. The blooms, which are cream-colored with fine pink or violet vertical stripes, can reach over 11 in (28 cm) long.

The flower gets its exaggerated length from a pair of modified sepals. The sepal is part of the green "cup" surrounding a flower. It usually helps protect the flower bud and support the full bloom, but is modified in many plant species so it appears to be a petal, as in irises, fuchsias, and columbines.

This bulbophyllum is an epiphyte that grows from the sides of trees so its unusual flowers hang downward. The flowers are dramatically displayed in a structure called an umbel. The term, derived from the Latin word for "parasol," refers to a group of short, flower-bearing stalks that flare out from the same point on a stem. The umbel of the long-petaled bulbophyllum holds groups of five to ten flowers on a plane with each other in a half circle. To some, the bizarre, trailing flowers hanging together in rings suggest ghostly chandeliers. But this otherworldly inflorescence is fleeting: the blooms last only a few days.

Cutting Garden

"Louise the Unfortunate" Rose

COMMON NAMES: 'Hume's Blush Tea-Scented China'

LATIN NAME: *Rosa* x *odorata*

MEANING: gentleness, sympathy

SEE PAGE 175

Cemeteries can be treasure troves for admirers of old roses. Planted to adorn the graves of loved ones, hardy antique roses often thrive and sprawl, sometimes living for hundreds of years. Some historic cemeteries in the United States feature roses brought over by European immigrants or carried west across the continent by pioneers. Cemeteries are a source of old roses unknown to modern horticulture and varieties thought to be completely lost. Like ancestral headstones, old roses often come with tantalizing stories.

One of these tales comes from a cemetery in Natchez, Mississippi. As the story goes, the intrepid Louise, a mail-order bride from New Orleans, arrived in Natchez on a steamboat to meet her fiancé and start a new life. But for some reason the marriage never occurred: in some accounts, she never found her fiancé; in others, he was already married. Though Louise knew no one in Natchez, she stayed, either because she couldn't afford the passage back home or because she was too embarrassed to return to New Orleans still unmarried.

At first, Louise was able to hold on to respectability, supporting herself by sewing and cleaning houses. Over time, she began to wait tables in Under-the-Hill, the seedy part of town. Eventually, she had to find work at one of several Under-the-Hill brothels. She died penniless, and, in some accounts, out on the streets. A man (who was either a doctor, a preacher, or a plantation owner and former client, depending on who tells the story) paid for Louise's funeral, interment, and headstone.

Today, her white marble headstone stands in the Natchez cemetery, with no dates and no surname. It says, simply, "Louise the Unfortunate." At some point, someone planted a rosebush near her grave with pale pink flowers, speculated to be 'Hume's Blush.' The rosebush hasn't been given an official name, but locals refer to it simply as "Louise the Unfortunate."

Allium

COMMON NAME: ornamental onion

SEE PAGE 178

LATIN NAME: *Allium hollandicum*

MEANING: prosperity, humility, patience

This globe of delicate florets atop a thick, smooth stalk is a glamorous cousin of the humble onion. The genus *Allium* includes onions, garlic, leeks, chives, and shallots. The word *allium* was used by the Romans to refer to garlic and thought to derive from the Greek word *aleo*, "to avoid," presumably because of the strong odor.

Allium varieties range from the dainty to the truly impressive, with flower umbels that can reach 10 in (25 cm) in diameter and stalks that grow to 4 ft (1.2 m) tall. Although the spherical allium in blues and purples is probably most familiar to flower gardeners, allium varieties can also be white or yellow, and their umbels can be cup shaped, semicircular, or pendulous.

The ornamental alliums we know today didn't appear on the European gardening scene until the late nineteenth century, when Russian naturalists collected them in Central Asia and brought them to the Imperial Botanical Garden in St. Petersburg. They soon appeared at Kew Gardens in London, and before long, English horticulturalists were developing spectacular hybrids.

Alliums are low maintenance, sometimes described as a "plant it and forget it" bulb. They attract pollinators like bees, butterflies, and hummingbirds, while repelling garden pests like deer, rabbits, squirrels, and woodchucks with the same sulfur compounds found in onions and garlic.

Alliums bloom in late spring, during the lull between the last of the tulips and the first of the roses. They bloom for up to three weeks; then the florets fade and drop from the umbel, leaving behind a starburst of floret stalks radiating from the stem at the center. Unpicked, it becomes a garden ornament; picked and dried, it will last months or more. Alas, for such an elegant flower, it has surprisingly sloppy foliage—long pointed leaves droop and then collapse around the base of the plant—so it's best to plant it among low-growing leafy neighbors that can help conceal the mess.

Black Hollyhock

COMMON NAMES: outhouse flower, alley orchid

LATIN NAME: *Alcea rosea*

MEANING: ambition, fruitfulness

SEE PAGE 183

Prolific and easy to care for, hollyhocks have been so common in home gardens in the last two or three centuries that they've picked up some unflattering associations. The common name, "outhouse flower," is the thanks this flower gets for a valuable service: before indoor plumbing, hollyhocks were often planted around outhouses because their tall stalks helped conceal the not especially appealing structures. Apparently, this use was so common that anyone looking for the outhouse could discreetly inquire as to the location of "the hollyhocks." The slightly less pejorative nickname "alley orchid" refers to the hollyhock's tendency to escape a garden and naturalize nearby.

The name "hollyhock" has somewhat uncertain origins. "Hock" comes from *hokke*, a variant of *hocc*, which is the Old English name for mallow, the hollyhock's family. "Holly" likely means "holy"; one legend has it that the flowers were brought to Europe during the Crusades, so "holy" refers to the Holy Land. Another theory is that "holy" refers to the flower's many medicinal applications: the plant has been used in folk medicine to treat inflammation, respiratory and digestive ailments, and skin rashes.

The hollyhock has also been used to treat childhood boredom. Generations of children made little hollyhock dolls using toothpicks and hollyhock flowers. A fully bloomed flower becomes the doll's skirt; a bud, its torso. The pièce de résistance is her head, made from a hollyhock bud with its calyx torn off. When the assemblage is set on its side, the furled petals give the doll an updo, the little spaces between the bud's petals resemble eyes, and the spot where the flower has been cut away from the stem suggests a mouth. The admittedly somewhat creepy doll is held together with a toothpick.

Hollyhock is the official flower for the thirteenth wedding anniversary, but when picking the hocks for your spouse's bouquet, it's probably more romantic to avoid the ones growing behind the old outhouse.

Itoh Peony

LATIN NAME: *Paeonia*

MEANING: shame, bashfulness

SEE PAGE 186

From Greek mythology to European folktales to Chinese iconography and Japanese fairy tales, peony lore presents an embarrassment of riches. The flower takes its name from Paeon, a Greek god of medicine and healing who treats both the god of war and the god of the underworld in Homer's *Iliad*. In the peony myth, Paeon studies under Asclepius, a master of the medical arts, and Asclepius becomes jealous of his student's talents. To save Paeon from his teacher's envious wrath, Zeus turns the student into a peony flower.

Before breathtaking Chinese ornamental peonies were introduced in the West, the flower was grown in Europe mostly for its healing properties. Peonies were believed to be an effective treatment for mental illness and epilepsy, and young children wore necklaces made from peony roots to ease the pain of teething and protect against convulsions. But, according to ancient superstitions, filling a peony prescription could be a dangerous task: the ancient Greek scholar Theophrastus reports the folk belief that those who pick peony seedpods in view of a woodpecker may have their eyes pecked out. Harvesting the root is supposedly no safer, since the woodpecker can somehow also inflict rectal injury.

The peony is the national flower of China and a ubiquitous motif in Chinese art. Traditionally grown in the gardens of imperial palaces, "the king of flowers" represents opulence, wealth, beauty, nobility, and honor. In Japan, the peony signifies courage, honor, and good fortune and has been given an only slightly less illustrious epithet, "the prime minister of flowers." But peonies in Japanese legend can have a darker side, as in a particularly spine-tingling tale called "The Peony Lantern," which features a beautiful woman, a lovelorn suitor, and several midnight trysts with a skeleton.

The Itoh peony featured here differs substantially from the balled-up pink and white peonies that many are familiar with; the Itoh's petals are looser, and its watercolor hues more subtle and sophisticated. It's named for its creator, Toichi Itoh, a twentieth-century Japanese botanist who was the first to successfully cross an herbaceous peony and a tree peony.

Opium Poppy

COMMON NAMES: breadseed poppy

LATIN NAME: *Papaver somniferum*

MEANING: endurance

SEE PAGE 191

The opium poppy has been used for its narcotic properties since 4000 B.C.E. The Latin species name, *somniferum*, literally means "sleep-bringing," an effect produced by alkaloids present in the flower's sap. The opium poppy's powerful narcotic effect has always been a double-edged sword: on one hand, the flower's anesthetic properties have eased the pain of millions of people over thousands of years, during most of which it was the only effective painkiller available. On the other hand, many of the pharmacological advances that refined and concentrated the drug for medical use also make it highly addictive.

When Friedrich Sertürner created the opium-derived morphine at the beginning of the nineteenth century, it was a wonder drug. Though practitioners had long used opioid tinctures to heal, morphine was far more powerful. Doctors began prescribing it for almost any complaint and ailment. This practice was made even more dangerous by the midcentury advent of the hypodermic needle, since the drug could then be injected directly into the veins of a patient.

In 1874, C. R. Alder Wright synthesized heroin; it was then used to help alleviate morphine addiction, and this "safer" alternative to morphine became a go-to for doctors prescribing medication for pain relief. In the nineteenth century, heroin was indicated for menstrual cramps, morning sickness, and "female hysteria." Available only to women who could afford ongoing medical care, morphine, and later heroin, were associated with upper-middle-class women. Unlike the opium smokers who patronized the seedy opium dens of London, San Francisco, and New York, ladies who received morphine injections from handsomely paid doctors were altogether more respectable.

Red Hot Poker

LATIN NAME: *Kniphofia*

SEE PAGE 194

This striking perennial produces dramatic spikes of bicolored flowers that reach from 2 to 6 ft (60 to 180 cm) tall. As the florets age, they change from dark red to orange to yellow. The florets at the bottom of the flower mature first, turning yellow and opening their petals. Over time, the yellow creeps up the hot poker, an engaging phenomenon to observe in the garden. The nectar-rich tubular florets are also appreciated by bees, butterflies, and hummingbirds.

Native to South Africa, red hot poker plants reached Europe in 1707, where they were grown in heated conservatories. In 1848, they were planted along the borders of Kew Gardens, and soon became popular additions to Victorian and then Edwardian gardens. Virginia Woolf and her husband grew red hot pokers in their garden at Monk's House, and she mentions the plants several times in her novel *To the Lighthouse*.

Kniphofia is named for Johann Hieronymus Kniphof, an eighteenth-century physician whose magnum opus *Botanica Pharmeceutica in originali* was the first large botanical work to incorporate "nature printing." This technique, originally developed in the fifteenth century, involved covering plant specimens with ink and pressing them between two pieces of paper. The process transferred very fine details like fibers and veins to the paper, in many cases with more accuracy than botanical illustrators of the time could achieve. Kniphof was very secretive about his own printing techniques, which remain mostly a mystery.

Witch Garden

Deadly Nightshade

COMMON NAMES: devil's herb, death cherries,

banewort, beautiful death

LATIN NAME: *Atropa belladonna*

MEANING: silence

SEE PAGE 199

Deadly nightshade, as its name suggests, is one of the Eastern Hemisphere's most toxic plants. It grows wild in much of the United States, and you'll often see this unassuming perennial with its small purple flowers and shiny black berries growing alongside other weeds in untended areas. *Belladonna*—"beautiful lady" in Italian—refers to the plant's cosmetic application: women used belladonna drops to dilate their pupils, an effect considered to be alluring. Its Latin name, *Atropa belladonna*, comes from one of the three fates, or Moirai, in Greek mythology. While the fates Clotho and Lachesis spin and measure a mortal's thread of life, Atropos, whose name means roughly "the inevitable," cuts it.

Accordingly, the toxin that makes belladonna so deadly is called atropine. It poisons by disrupting the parasympathetic nervous system; the body can't regulate involuntary processes like sweating, breathing, and heart rate, causing illness and even death. Belladonna has been used to poison arrow tips and, legend has it, to murder Roman emperors. The plant's black berries are especially dangerous for children, since they resemble blueberries and taste sweet.

Belladonna has long been associated with witches and is fabled to be a main ingredient in flying ointment, a salve that witches apply to their broomsticks to give them the power of flight. One theory is that this association is rooted in early experimentation with hallucinatory recreational drugs. Ergot, belladonna, henbane, and mandrake were all known to cause hallucinations, and people may have found that the best way to safely consume the hallucinatory compounds was to absorb them via mucous membranes. Ointments were made containing these substances and, the theory goes, applied to a broom handle. The figure of the witch naked astride her broom might have been inspired by the intrepid thrill seeker tripping out by means of the most effective tools at hand.

Cobra Lily

COMMON NAME: pitcher plant

LATIN NAME: *Sarracenia leucophylla*

SEE PAGE 202

Often called pitcher plants in the nursery trade and cobra lilies by florists, *Sarracenia leucophylla* are carnivorous plants that grow in sunny bogs, swamps, and other wetlands. They have adapted to grow in poor soil by producing pitfall traps that allow them to collect nutrients from prey insects.

Attracted by a frilled white or red pitcher lid masquerading as a flower, a fly alights on a pitcher's lid. It soon finds that the pitcher has secreted nectar bribes around the edges of the lid, and that there is even more nectar to be had on the lid's underside. The fly follows this sweet trail until it finds itself gobbling nectar while hanging upside down directly over the pitcher. One false move, and it falls straight down into the trap.

Once inside, the fly's wings are soaked in digestive fluid. Weakened and, like most winged insects, unable to fly straight up, the captured fly tries again and again to launch itself at an upward angle and instead repeatedly crashes against the walls of the pitcher. When it tries to crawl up the sides of the tube, it encounters a slippery coating. Beyond that are tiny hairs that grow downward, creating a gauntlet the exhausted fly can't overcome. The insect falls into the pool of fluid to be

dissolved and digested; eventually, its body will provide the plant with essential nitrogen and phosphorus.

Some species of cobra lily use insects as a component of their digestive liquid. Trapped ants provide not only a nutritious meal but also a dose of formic acid, the chemical that makes ant bites so painful. The formic acid helps lower the pH of the fluid, making it even more effective at breaking down prey. Other cobra lily species host tiny larvae in their acidic pools, which eat captured insects and then excrete nutrients the plant can easily absorb.

These fascinating carnivores are imperiled both by habitat loss and by horticulturalists selling the plants and cut flowers. Before you buy either, it's a good idea to make sure they've been farmed rather than foraged.

Amethyst Deceiver

COMMON NAMES: red cabbage mushroom,

common deceiver

LATIN NAME: *Laccaria amethystina*

SEE PAGE 114

Although its sinister-sounding name and unusual purple color suggest that this plant might be found in a witch's brew, the beautiful amethyst deceiver is actually a pretty innocuous little toadstool. Like amethyst, the gemstone mineral they're named for, these mushrooms come in a range of purples. As the mushrooms age and become dry, their purple fades to a pale grayish brown, making them harder to distinguish from other brownish and purplish mushrooms—thus the name "deceiver."

The darkest thing that can be said about amethyst deceivers is that they are little vampires. Growing among the leaf detritus beneath a tree (often beech), a mushroom detects a tree root. In response, the mushroom produces tiny filaments called hyphae that grow into the root, effectively turning the tree root into a straw that allows the mushrooms to suck nutrients from the tree. This behavior isn't really as nefarious as it sounds—this ectomycorrhizal relationship is also beneficial for the tree: the deceiver helps the tree absorb water and provides it with essential nutrients.

The amethyst deceiver is considered edible, but it can bioaccumulate arsenic, soaking the pollutant from the soil like a sponge. And mushroom hunters need to be careful, as it's dangerously similar to other purple mushrooms that are toxic, like the lilac fibrecap. While rarely lethal, the lilac fibrecap contains enough of the toxin muscarine to produce an extremely unpleasant bout of abdominal pain and nausea. As with all mushrooms, amethyst deceivers should be verified by a mushroom expert before they're consumed.

If you do verify that you have a basket of amethyst deceivers on your hands, you're in for a visual as well as a gustatory treat: the mushrooms keep their purple color when cooked, making for a lovely presentation.

King Protea

COMMON NAMES: giant protea, honeypot, king sugar bush

LATIN: *Protea cynaroides*

MEANING: diversity, courage, hope, change

SEE PAGE 207

In 1736, Carl Linnaeus, the father of botanical taxonomy, named the protea after a sea god. In Greek mythology, Proteus, the son of Poseidon and the older brother of Triton, was a shape-shifter and fortune-teller. When mortals came to hear their fortunes, Proteus turned himself into a series of different animals in order to evade their grasp. Only a person who could hold him through all his changes of form could force him to reveal the future.

Linnaeus gave the plant Proteus's name because of the highly varied forms it can take: there are proteas that look like pincushions, paintbrushes, and artichokes. Others have shapes so eccentric they're difficult to describe. King proteas also seem to shape-shift as they bloom. The closed flower head almost resembles a large, scaly dragon egg, but instead of containing a baby dragon, the pink petal-like bracts open to reveal a fuzzy white center made up of the plant's true flowers. When the flower head is fully open, the bracts form a crown around the flowers, thus the name king protea.

Modern proteas are descendants of proteas that existed during the Cretaceous Period. They're drought resistant, adapted to survive wildfires, and long-lived—a protea plant can last a century. But even the toughest protea can be susceptible to a deformity called witches' broom, which changes the structure of the flower head. Its buds are stimulated to divide and subdivide, resulting in a dense clump of plant matter. In a king protea, a stem struck by witches' broom is a grotesque clump of tiny protea flower heads squashed together and growing into and out of each other.

Snake's Head Fritillary

COMMON NAMES: leper's bells, leper lily, Lazarus bell, dead man's bells

LATIN NAME: *Fritillaria meleagris*

MEANING: persecution

SEE PAGE 210

This plant's Latin name, *Fritillaria meleagris*, refers to the resemblance between the checked pattern on the fritillaria's petals and the feathers of a guinea hen; its common names, however, hint at the darker associations of a bloom that poet Vita Sackville-West once called "a sinister little flower, in the mournful colour of decay."

The common name "leper's bells" refers to the medieval practice of lepers carrying bells and clappers. Some historians believe that, to reduce contagion, people with leprosy were required by law to carry these instruments to warn those without leprosy of their presence. Others argue that, since leprosy damages the vocal cords, the bells and clappers made it possible for lepers to "call" to passersby for alms. This association of the flower with leprosy is also reflected in the plant's other common name, "Lazarus bell": in the New Testament, Lazarus, the unofficial patron saint of lepers, was a miserable beggar whose sores were licked by dogs and who, in death, found favor with God. Lepers were sometimes referred to as lazars, casting them as virtuous sufferers worthy of care.

The flower was rumored to have acquired its downward-facing habit at Calvary, where, the story goes, snake's head fritillaries growing nearby witnessed the crucifixion and hung their heads in sadness. But the flower also has some positive associations; for some it symbolized the wonder of creation, since the evenly checkered petals seemed to reveal the perfection of divine order, which sixteenth-century botanist and herbalist John Gerard described as "chequered most strangely: wherein . . . the Creator of all things, hath kept a very wonderful order, surpassing (as in all other things) the curiousest painting that Art can set down."

It's believed that *Fritillaria meleagris* was assigned the meaning "persecution" in the language of flowers to honor its discoverer, Noel Capron, one of many Protestant French Huguenots killed by Catholic mob violence in the St. Bartholomew's massacre of 1572. The nineteenth-century horticultural writer Henry Phillips, who assigned this meaning, recommended that the flower be planted in every garden as a reminder that "by persecuting others, we lessen our own portion of happiness."

Corpse Flower

COMMON NAMES: titan arum

LATIN NAME: *Amorphophallus titanum*

SEE PAGE 215

Native to Sumatra and Java, the full-grown corpse flower has a 10 ft (3 m) center spadix surrounded by a spathe that forms a pleated skirtlike structure. At the bottom of the spadix, deep inside the flower, are rings of small flowers. That makes the corpse flower an inflorescence (an entire flowering structure) rather than a single flower.

It takes eight to ten years for the "flower" to bloom. When it does, the spathe opens up, revealing that it is dark red inside and textured to resemble meat. The plant's namesake smell is released, an odor that chemical analysis has found to be a mélange of rotten fish, sweaty socks, mothballs, limburger cheese, excrement, and a sweet floral scent. As it blooms, the tip of the spadix warms to about 98°F (37°C), intensifying the odor and causing it to waft as the warm air rises.

The flower's stench draws pollinators, flesh flies, and carrion beetles in search of a place to lay their eggs. As an insect moves around the plant in search of the source of the rotting meat smell, its legs become covered in pollen; it's then ready to pollinate the next corpse flower it encounters.

Its Latin name means "giant misshapen penis." David Attenborough, whose team first captured on film the flowering and pollination of the corpse flower for the BBC, coined the name "titan arum." He feared that his audience might be scandalized by repeated use of the flower's Latin name; his tamer alternative has become one of the most common names for the plant.

Corpse flower bloomings attract thousands of curious visitors to botanical gardens. For garden staff, though, this is no time to sit back and admire. Pollen is collected, packed, and shipped to pollinate corpse flowers in other botanical gardens. Although they are doing the work of flesh flies and carrion beetles, these gardeners seem to have nothing but fondness for their enchantingly repulsive charges, even giving them names: Trudy lives in the Berkeley Botanical Garden, Spike and Alice in the Chicago Botanic Garden, Rosie in the Tucson Botanical Garden, and Morticia in the Franklin Park Zoo in Boston.

Foundational Tools
and Techniques

SELECTING CREPE PAPER

Crepe paper comes in three basic weights. Heavy crepe, also called florist crepe, is made in Europe and China. European heavy crepe comes in 160 and 180 gram weights, which are so similar you might not notice a difference. Heavy crepe imported from China is lower in quality and lacks European crepe's crisp grain, but you can use it strategically to produce softer petals with less stretching. Both European and Chinese heavy crepe have large crinkles that give the paper a lot of stretch and body. Because the grain is so pronounced, it must be stretched out most of the way to achieve a smooth, realistic petal surface.

Doublette crepe is a medium-weight crepe with a different color on each side. It doesn't have as much stretch as heavy crepe, so it can't be shaped as dramatically, but its finer grain produces very realistic petals, with enough body to support blooms that need more structure.

Fine crepe paper comes in three weights: 32 gram, 60 gram, and extra fine. The 32-gram crepe is similar in weight to tissue paper. Its grain is very fine, though it does have some stretch. The 60 gram is similar but has greater stretch and a slightly coarser grain. Somewhat confusingly, extra-fine crepe is the heaviest of the fine crepes and also the stretchiest. It has a slightly matte surface, so it isn't quite as lustrous as the other fine crepes.

CUTTING PETALS

The grain of crepe paper runs in only one direction, up and down, parallel to the roll or fold. This means that it stretches only horizontally. Because most petals are shaped by stretching ruffles across the top, or cups across the bottom, you'll almost always cut petals with the grain running from the base to the tip of the petal. I've included an arrow in the templates to show which way the grain runs, so when positioning templates on crepe, make sure that the grain runs parallel to the arrow.

I've drawn two kinds of petal templates. The half-petal templates that include one straight side with a dotted line are meant to be cut on a fold, so the half petal opens out into a full petal when the crepe is unfolded. Make sure that the folded crepe is long enough to contain the whole height of the template and wide enough to contain the width. Also be sure to align the fold with the dotted line on the template. To cut multiple petals at a time, you can accordion fold the crepe—again, just make sure that the folds line up with the dotted line.

For whole petal templates, simply place them on top of one or more layers of crepe (making sure the grain is running in the same direction as the arrow) and cut around the template.

CUPPING PETALS

Hold the petal with two hands, positioning your thumbs on top of it, meeting in the center of the area you want to cup. Keep the pads of your thumbs flat, and pinch the petal between your thumbs on the front and fingers on the back. Stretch the paper between your thumbs, moving outward horizontally but also forward with your thumbs and backward with your fingers. Stretch the area specified in the project instructions, making sure not to stretch the outside edge. Otherwise, you'll end up with a larger, flat petal.

Practice with some test petals. Try to actually tear the petal to get a sense of what level of force is too much. It's better to stretch the same area gently a few times than with one strong motion, which can leave dents in the petals.

Once the petal is cupped, run it between your thumb and forefinger to smooth out any bumpy areas.

CURLING PETALS

To curl a petal, grip it between your thumb and a scissor blade, and scrape out to the edge of the petal. As with cupping, it's better to do several gentle scrapes, rather than one very hard scrape that may damage the paper. For a more gentle curl, use a dowel; for a very small, tight curl, try a skewer.

STRETCHING PETALS

To stretch (or ruffle) petals, just stretch the crepe across the top edge of the petal. Generally, I find that it looks more realistic to stretch just the very upper edge, rather than starting farther down on the petal. Different weights of crepe will create different levels of ruffle depending on grain. As you're familiarizing yourself with crepe paper, experiment with ruffling petals in multiple weights.

STRETCHING CREPE PAPER AROUND A SHAPE

You can stretch crepe paper around ball and egg shapes, creating a smooth surface. Use the measurements in the project instructions to cut the strip of crepe that will cover the cotton or foam ball form. Place the cotton or foam ball in the middle of the strip, both vertically and horizontally. Bring both sides of the strip to meet at the opposite side of the ball, and pull the crepe paper snugly around the ball. Reopen the strip and remove the ball. You'll see the ball's imprint in the section of crepe that was wrapped around it. Dot the concave side of the stretched crepe with glue and then put the ball back in place. Press the upper and lower edge of the strip down onto the ball. Snip the crepe so that you're left with a narrow overlap, dot glue on the seam, and press it to one side.

CRINKLING

Lay the crepe in front of you on a smooth surface, so that the grain runs horizontally. Place your fingertips about 1 in/2.5 cm from the edge of the paper closest to you. Place your thumbs on the edge of the paper closest to you, and your fingers about 1 in/2.5 cm forward from your thumbs. Use your thumbs to inch the paper toward your fingers, dragging the paper along the smooth surface. This will create little pleats. When your thumbs and fingers touch, leave your thumbs in place, and lift your fingertips and set them down about 1 in/2.5 cm forward. Repeat until you've gathered the whole piece into pleats.

COMMON PETAL CONFIGURATIONS

To attach a petal, dot the base of the petal with glue up to the glue line—a line I've included across the bottom end of many of the templates to show how high up to apply the glue. Dot sparingly but thoroughly; aim for more coverage with less glue. Apply the petal to the stem where indicated in the instructions. For light- and medium-weight crepes, press the petal for a second or two. For heavy crepe, press for three to five seconds.

ONE ROW OF FOUR PETALS

To add one row of four petals, place the first two petals opposite each other. Place the second two petals in the spaces on either side of the first two petals.

ONE ROW OF FIVE PETALS

Place the first two petals next to each other on one side of the flower. Place a third flower directly opposite the "V" where the first two petals meet each other. Place the remaining two petals in the spaces on either side of the third petal.

SIX PETALS IN TWO ROWS OF THREE PETALS

Attach three petals evenly around the center. In the spaces between these petals, attach the remaining three petals.

FLOWERS WITH MULTIPLE ROWS

Distribute the petals evenly around the center. Individual project instructions indicate how much to overlap the petals. As you add more rows, you'll add the first petal of a new row next to the last petal in the previous row, so you end up with a continuous spiral. Make sure to glue the petals close to the base of the previous row's petals, just slightly below, so you don't end up drifting down the stem.

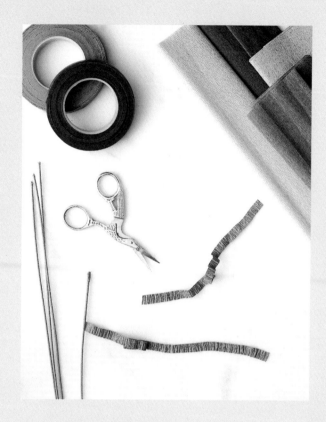

MAKING CONFETTI-STYLE STAMENS

Follow the project instructions to cut a fringe rectangle and a confetti rectangle. Fold the fringe rectangle lengthwise along the line shown on the fringe rectangle template. Cut a fringe across the rectangle. Finer is better, but don't stress about it. When the whole rectangle is fringed, check the template to see if there is a diagonal line across the bottom half of the template. If so, cut along this line.

Fringe the confetti rectangle in the same way you fringed the first rectangle. Then turn it 90 degrees. Hold the rectangle over a plate and cross-cut, creating confetti. Squirt glue onto a plate. Dip the stamens in the glue and then in the pile of confetti. Allow to dry.

You can apply the confetti to the fringes before or after you attach the fringes to the stem. Each project will recommend which technique to use.

STEM WRAPPING

Wrapping a wire flower stem with crepe paper helps hide the bottoms of petals and creates a smooth, realistic-looking stem. I prefer to use 18-gauge cloth-covered stem wire for most flowers because the weight is flexible enough to pose easily, but not too floppy to hold its shape, and the paper adheres really well to the cloth cover, rather than sliding around on a bare wire. Stem wire comes in a standard 18 in/46 cm length. Unless noted, the projects in this book use standard-length wire. When you use wire snips to trim stem wire, consider wearing eye protection.

I use crepe paper rather than floral tape for most stem constructions because I find it easier to work with, and I like to be able to create stems in just about any color, rather than being limited to floral tape colors. You can use any weight of crepe paper for this,

but my favorite is Lia Griffith's extra-fine crepe (made in Germany by Werola). It's both very light and very stretchy, and it doesn't tear as easily as some other lightweight crepes.

Cut the stem-wrapping strips across the grain of the crepe paper. They should be ¼ in/6 mm wide and between 6 and 10 in/15 and 25 cm long. (Very long strips can be hard to wrangle.) I call these stem strips. If you're wrapping the base of a flower, begin by dotting glue on the first 2 in/5 cm of a stem strip. Attach the strip beginning at the back of the flower. Wrap twice around the base of the petals, stretching the strip slightly to press them against the stem. Then, holding the strip at a 45-degree angle to the stem wire, spiral down the stem, gently stretching the strip to create a smooth surface. Once you've used up the section of the strip that was dotted with glue, dot the unwrapped stem with glue. Continue to wrap down the stem until you reach the bottom of the wire, and

snip off any excess stem strip. If the strip tears as you're wrapping, just begin again with a new strip ¼ in/6 mm above the place on the stem where the first strip tore.

When you reach the bottom of the stem, cut away the excess strip and make sure the part of the strip that covers the end of the wire is glued securely in place. For thicker stems, repeat this process with additional strips until you've reached your desired thickness.

For very thick stems, use polyvinyl tubing slipped over the stem wire, cut approximately 1½ in/4 cm shorter than the wire. Wrap the tubing just as you would stem wire. If the tubing won't stay straight, insert additional stem wire into the tube. To secure the tubing in place over the stem, bend the wires at the bottom back 180 degrees so they fold back against the bottom of the tubing.

MITERED LEAF

We can use the grain of the crepe to create a realistic-looking leaf by cutting and gluing it so the grain of each side meets the centerline of the leaf to create a "V." First, cut a rectangle using the dimensions provided in the project instructions. Cut the rectangle from the bottom right-hand corner up to the upper left-hand corner. This will produce two triangles. Flip one of the triangles vertically, and place them on the table side by side, with the diagonal cuts parallel to each other. Dot a ¼-in-/6-mm-wide strip along the diagonal edge of the left triangle with glue.

Imagine that the two triangles on your work surface form an open book. Close the "book" by placing the left triangle on top of the right, with all the edges lined up. Press along the diagonal to set the glue and allow it to dry. Once it's dry, open up the book, pressing one of the triangles completely flat over the seam to create a crease. Make sure the two triangles create a chevron where they meet down the middle. This mitered packet is right-side up when the grain runs upward from the middle.

Close the "book" again and place the half-leaf template so the straight edge aligns with the crease. (Make sure that the template and the packet are both right-side up.) Cut around the template to create the leaf.

Open the leaf and press it flat. Wrap the leaf stem, following the project instructions. To determine how much of the stem to dot with glue, place the stem between the side of the leaf and the folded-over seam so it's three-quarters of the way up the leaf. Dot this length of the stem with glue and glue it behind the seam, orienting the glued side so the stem adheres to the seam rather than the back of the leaf. Dot a tiny amount of glue on the bottom edge of the leaf in the center and press it against the wrapped stem to anchor it.

EMBOSSING TOOLS

I use embossing tools and a ⅛ in/3 mm craft foam sheet to create curled edges and ribbed patterns on cardstock. Follow the project instructions and, if provided, the embossing pattern on the template. Place the cardstock on the foam sheet and use the embossing tool to draw a line on the cardstock, pressing the paper into the foam. Experiment by embossing with different levels of force to find the embossing depth you like best.

EMBOSSED PATTERNS

If applicable, use the pattern on the template as a general guideline for applying the embossing (there's no need to transfer the pattern exactly). For heavier lines on the pattern, use a ¼ in/6 mm embossing tool; for lighter lines, use a ¹⁄₁₆ in/2 mm or similarly fine tool.

EMBOSSED EDGES & POINTS

To create three-dimensional leaves, place the leaf face down and use the ¼ in/6 mm embossing tool to trace just inside the outer edges of the leaf. Once the whole leaf is embossed, use your fingers to bend back the cardstock. Aim for a smoothly bent edge.

To add a point to a leaf with embossed edges, make sure you've embossed all the way up to the point on either side. Pinch the tip, applying pressure evenly on either side of the point.

ACRYLIC WASH

To achieve the powdery surface of some succulents and cacti, I use a wisteria light purple acrylic craft paint. I've also experimented with pale pinks, blues, and yellows to good effect, but the wisteria purple is my go-to for this application. Dilute the paint in water using the ratio specified in the project instructions. Use a foam paintbrush to swipe paint from one end of the paper to the other. If the paper has a grain, paint with the grain. Try to keep the coat fairly even and not too streaky.

For a more pronounced powdery look, add a second coat. (The second coat also helps conceal any streaks, so if you have an uneven first coat, opt for a second coat.)

OVER-DYE

I use alcohol inks for customizing the color of my crepe paper. These inks aren't absorbed by the paper the way water is absorbed, so using them doesn't distort the grain. You can first dye paper to cut petals from, or cut the petals first and dye them afterward. You can also dip dye parts of the petal.

You don't need to soak petals in the dye, and they don't take very long to dry. Once they're completely dry, they won't bleed onto other surfaces. To create pastel colors, dilute the ink in 99-percent isopropyl alcohol. Make sure you have appropriate ventilation, and be forewarned that the ink will stain anything it comes into contact with, including fingers, so I recommend wearing gloves.

BLENDING

Alcohol ink markers are ideal for creating color gradation because they're so easy to blend without wetting the crepe and ruining its texture (as water-based inks can do). Hard lines can be softened using a clear blending marker (Copic Colorless Blender is one of my most frequently used tools), but I especially love creating a streaky, two-toned effect using two colors. First, I draw streaks in a darker shade radiating out from the middle of the petal base; then, using a lighter shade, I color the entire petal. If any of the streaks are still too stark, I use the lighter shade to smooth them into the overall petal color for a more natural effect. The greater the difference between the first and second markers, the more pronounced the streaks will appear.

FOUNDATIONAL TOOLS
AND TECHNIQUES

SPECKLING

Before adding any speckles, test the pen on a scrap of the paper stock you'll be speckling. If the ink feathers very much—spreading up and down the crepe away from the dots—try a different pen or marker.

Plant and flower speckles are usually a combination of smaller and larger dots, which are usually denser in one central area and become more sparse farther away. I find it easiest to evenly apply them by dotting the area I want to speckle with small dots and then enlarging some of those dots as a second step. You can enlarge dots by holding the pen to the paper longer or by drawing them as a larger circle on top of a small dot.

Don't worry about making things too even or avoiding any feathering. Some irregularities will improve the speckles, making them look more natural.

COLORING EDGES

To add a very fine stroke of color to the petal or leaf edges, gently scrape the tip of a marker or felt-tip pen along the edge of the petal, rather than trying to draw a line across the front of the petal at the tip. The longer you hold the marker to the paper, the more ink will wick into it and the wider the line will be.

PASTEL

I use PanPastel, a powdery pastel that goes on like eye shadow. It's completely dry, so it doesn't wet the crepe, and because you can brush it on lightly, it doesn't warp delicate paper or settle unevenly.

For allover color, I apply the PanPastel with a wedge-shaped latex cosmetic sponge, simply swiping it across the petals. My favorite application for this technique is creating rich, velvety-looking petals. For example, a deep red or magenta over black crepe creates a gorgeous deep oxblood.

I use a soft brush (a cheap blusher brush is perfect) to apply PanPastel in areas where the pastel might lodge in folds if swiped across using a sponge. For example, the anthurium spadix is wrapped in floral tape. If I were to try to brush across its surface, the pastel would concentrate in the edges of the floral tape. But if I use a soft brush to dab the pastel up and down the surface, I get a nice even tone.

SPRAY COLOR

I use Design Master Colortool and Tint IT spray paints. These are lightweight sprays that florists use to spray color on plants. You can also experiment with other types of spray paint.

To create ombre effects, hold the can between 12 and 18 in/30.5 and 46 cm from the paper and spray stripes across it, making sure the stripes are far enough apart to fit the template. You can place the template higher or lower on the stripe, depending on the concentration of color you're looking for. You can also layer the spray paint, spraying a stripe underneath the first, overlapping by about 30 percent.

It's best to use spray paints outside (with a mask), because it smells like bug spray. Let the paper dry completely and, if possible, give it a day to air outside. The odor will diminish significantly after twelve hours and fade completely within a week or two.

PART III

Making the Flowers

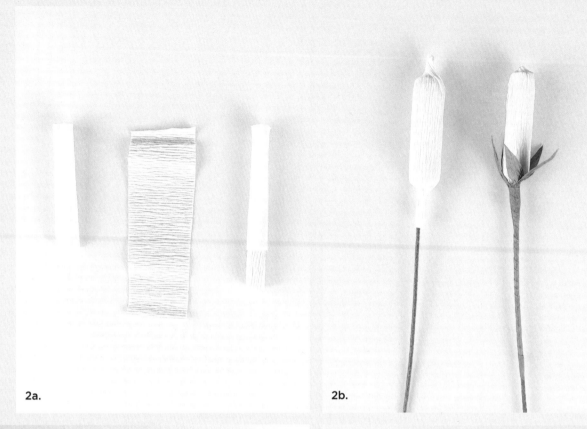

2a.

2b.

3b.

3c.

Foxglove

SEE PAGE 16

There's an empty lot near my home that puts on a spectacular foxglove display every year. One year, I nabbed one of the stalks and took it apart, studying the petal shapes, floret placement, and stem structure.

1. **Prepping the crepe for the greenery**

   a. Cut a 10 in/25 cm square from the Ivory crepe and, following the instructions on page 99, spray the square with the Basil paint until you have an even, opaque coat. This is the paper you'll use for the calyx, bracts, and stem strips. When you cut the calyx pieces and bracts, you'll stretch sections of the painted paper so they're completely uncrinkled, and then cut the pieces. Using wire snips and eye protection, cut thirteen 3 in/7.5 cm lengths of stem wire.

2. **Making the buds**

   a. Cut a template A piece from the Vanilla crepe. Dot glue on the edge of one long side of the piece and attach it to the opposite edge, forming the piece into a tube. To help this tube keep its shape, we're going to stuff it with a rolled strip of heavy crepe. From the White heavy crepe, cut a 1 by 4½ in/2.5 by 11 cm strip (the bud template strips will be 1¼ in/3 cm wide). Loosely roll this strip until it's thick enough to fit snugly in the tube, and trim off any extra. Insert the roll into the tube until there is only ½ in/12 mm of tube extending beyond the white heavy crepe roll.

   b. Dot glue all around the inside of this ½ in/12 mm section at the front of the tube, and twist. When the glue is dry, snip the twisted section, leaving a small amount of glued twist to keep the tube closed. Dot glue inside the opposite end of the tube, right up to the rolled crepe inside. Insert a wire into the middle of the roll of crepe (for the first three buds, this will be an 18 in/46 cm wire; for the remaining bud, this will be a 3 in/7.5 cm wire). Gather the tube around the wire. Cut five calyx pieces, using template C and the sprayed crepe, and distribute them evenly behind the bud. Cut stem strips from the sprayed crepe and use the instructions on page 92 for wrapping stems. Repeat to make three template B buds. For the A bud, wrap from behind the calyx to 1 in/2.5 cm down the wire. Wrap the template B buds behind the calyx and stop ¾ in/2 cm down the wire. Repeat to make two more template B buds.

3. **Making the flowers**

   a. You will use pairs of templates to make florets in three sizes: three small (templates E and F), three medium (templates G and H), and at least three large (templates I and J). The first template listed in each pair will be the top of the "bell," and the second will be the bottom. Cut the pieces from the Vanilla crepe, following the instructions

SUPPLIES

Scissors

Ivory extra-heavy crepe

Design Master Colortool spray paint in Basil (676)

Vanilla extra-fine crepe

Aleene's Original Tacky Glue

White or Off-White heavy crepe

Eye protection

Wire snips

22-gauge cloth-covered stem wire

Tsukineko Memento Dual Tip Marker in Sweet Plum (PM-506)

Templates (page 222)

on page 87 for cutting petals on a fold. Follow the speckling instructions on page 98 to speckle three F template pieces using the plum marker. Gently stretch the scalloped edges of both the E and F pieces, and following the instructions on page 88, lightly scissor curl the edges back. The F piece should be curled away from the speckled side.

b. Lay an E piece on the table. Using the dotted lines on the templates as a guide, dot glue from one of the dotted lines on the E piece out to the side of the bell, stopping near the top of the template where the dotted line stops. Lay one of the speckled F pieces onto the glue, speckle-side up, overlapping so the edge of the F piece lines up with the dotted line on the E piece (the speckled piece will be on top). Fold the speckled piece in half vertically. Dot the opposite side of the E piece with glue in the same way you did the first side. Fold the E piece in half and press the glued section onto the other side of the F piece.

c. Stick your finger into the bell up to the glue line and twist. Remove your finger, untwist the end, and insert a 3 in/7.5 cm wire so it falls just below the glue line. Stick your finger back inside the bell and gather the paper below the glue line around the wire.

d. Cut five calyx pieces using template C and distribute evenly around the foxglove bell. Wrap from behind the calyx to ¾ in/2 cm down the wire.

e. Repeat steps 3a through 3d to make two more small bells, three medium bells, and three large bells.

4. Building the stem

a. The first three buds have been built around a full 18 in/46 cm long stem of the wire. The template A bud goes on top. Place two of the template B buds 1 in/2.5 cm below on either side of the A bud, matching up the point on the three wires where the stem wrapping stops. Wrap the three wires together for ¾ in/2 cm.

b. Cut twelve bract pieces from the sprayed green crepe using template D. Glue one on either side of the two B buds so that they hit the stem just below the point where the bud's stem meets the main stem. For the bud on the left, place the bract on the left side of the stem. For the bud on the right side, place the bract on the right.

c. Place the next B bud below the previous B buds, lining it up with the A bud in the middle of the stem. Attach this B bud to the stem so that the

place where the stem wrap stops on the main stem meets the place where the stem wrap stops on the B bud. Wrap these together for ¾ in/2 cm. Add a bract directly beneath the point where the bud stem meets up with the main stem. You will add bracts in this way for all the buds and bells on the stem.

d. Next, add a small bell on the right side of the stem, lining up the point where the wrapping ends on the floret stem and the main stem. Wrap these together for ¾ in/2 cm. Repeat, adding a small bell on the left and then in the middle. Next, add three medium bells, applied in the same way and in the same sequence. Then add three large bells in the same way and in the same sequence.

e. You can continue adding more of the largest florets if you like. Wherever you plan to stop, remember that the last three florets you attach should be built on 18 in/46 cm wire. Add these in the same way you added all the others. Wrap to the bottom of the stem.

5. Finishing the foxglove

a. Gently bend all the floret wires to a 30-degree angle. The two template B buds just under the top bud should be at more of a 45-degree angle, while the A bud should be closer to 90 degrees. Wearing eye protection and using the wire snips, trim the foxglove stem to your preferred length.

b. Stick your fingers into any collapsed bells to restore their shape.

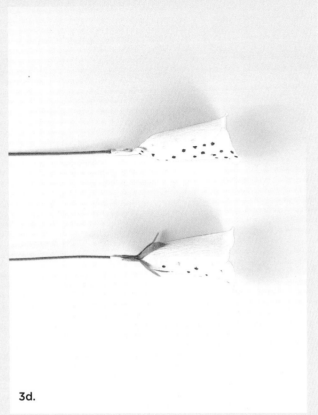

3d.

4a.

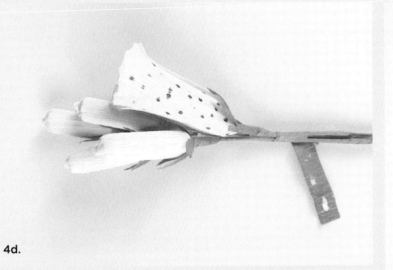

4d.

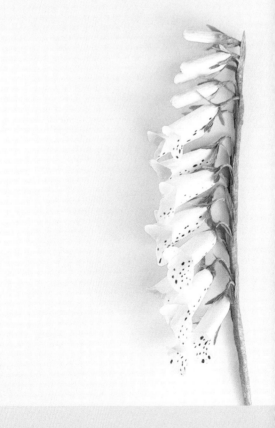

Jack-in-the-Pulpit

SEE PAGE 19

Jacks come with a wide variety of markings: some are pale green with white stripes, some are dark red from the hood to the body and then fade to green, and some are black with very pale green stripes. For this one, you'll use very dark red crepe covered in lines from a green-colored pencil and reverse the paper for color variation between flowers.

1. Making the spadix

a. Following the instructions on page 92, wrap the wire with the floral tape, stretching as you wrap to activate the adhesive and to create a smooth surface. Wrap from the tip of the wire to 3 in/7.5 cm down the wire and back up again. Repeat until the spadix is just under ¼ in/6 mm thick. Cut the tape at the bottom of the spadix and glue the end into place. Mold the tip of the spadix to make it smooth and tapered.

2. Making the spathe

a. Following the instructions on page 87 for cutting a template on a fold, cut one template A piece from the doublette. Turn the A piece so the darker side is showing. Start at the edge of the A piece, and use the colored pencil to draw lines up and down the template. To make a solid, saturated line, I scribble a small section of the line multiple times and then move up to the next section, making sure to keep my pencil sharp.

b. When you get to the section under the hood, skip it, and continue to draw lines toward the opposite side of the A piece. Draw the lines on the hood of the A piece. Extend each of the lines at the bottom of the hood all the way down the body and fill in any sections that are sparse so the parallel lines look uniform across the body part of the A piece.

c. Flip the piece over to the lighter side and repeat for the markings on the hood that extend down the body, but extend them by only 1 in/2.5 cm for each line. Add short parallel lines along the back of what will be the tube. (You're trying to draw lines on only the parts inside the tube that can be seen when the plant is glued together.)

d. Dot glue along the edge of one of the sides of the A piece, and gently curl the sides to the middle so they overlap and are glued shut.

e. Following the instructions on page 88 for scissor curling, gently curl the top half of the hood toward the light side. Use the dowel to curl the "neck" section of the hood forward. If additional curling is necessary to pitch the hood forward over the tube, scissor curl the neck area.

SUPPLIES

18-gauge cloth-covered stem wire

Black floral tape

Scissors

Aleene's Original Tacky Glue

Sangria or Aubergine doublette crepe

Prismacolor colored pencil in Apple Green (3343), well sharpened

¼ in/6 mm dowel

Cypress extra-fine crepe

Template (page 222)

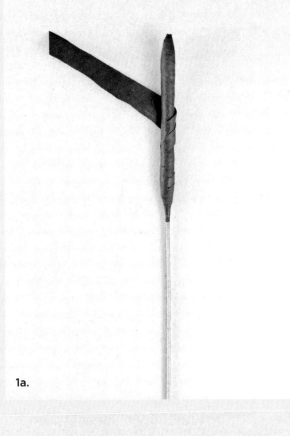

1a.

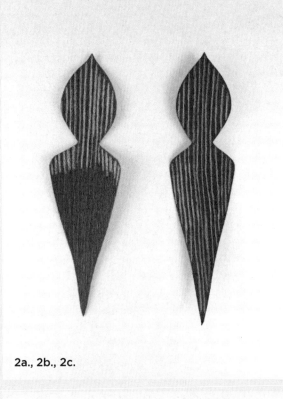

2a., 2b., 2c.

2d., 2e.

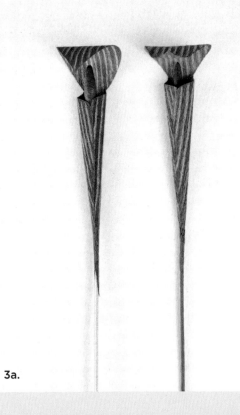

3a.

3. Assembling the jack

a. Thread the spadix down through the middle of the jack, so the tip of the spadix sticks out almost all the way to the roof of the spathe. Using stem strips cut from the Cypress crepe, wrap the bottom ¼ in/6 mm of the spathe tube to the wire, then wrap to the bottom of the stem. Readjust any parts of the tube that may have been disarranged during the wrapping.

b. If you're making multiple jacks, try alternating which side of the paper faces outward.

1a.

1c.

1d.

2a.

Log with Moss & Lichen

SEE PAGE 20

I left my log on the floor by my work area for some silly reason, and, naturally, one of my children stepped on it. But I actually think it improved the log, making it seem looser and more decayed inside. I don't recommend standing on *your* log, but you might try pressing it down on a table so it isn't so rounded and perky.

Note: For the extra-fine crepe, any brown will do; I just like the way the nonmetallic side of the metallic copper crepe looks with the latte heavy crepe.

1. **Making the log**

   a. Unroll the Latte crepe and cut off a 5 ft/1.5 m length. Cut a steeply angled, jagged fringed edge on both long ends of the crepe (it's not important to follow a specific pattern). Stretch out the jagged edges of the crepe on both ends. Following the instructions on page 90 for crinkling paper, crinkle the stretched-out portions on both ends, twisting and untwisting individual small sections.

   b. Loosely roll up the log. If it's too thick for your liking, unroll some of the latte crepe and cut it off. If it feels too skinny, prep additional lengths and just keep wrapping them around the log. Firmly twist together all the triangular parts on each end into one big bundle and then untwist them.

   c. To make the bark, cut a length of the Copper crepe long enough to wrap all the way around the log with a 1 in/2.5 cm overlap. Rip an irregular edge across the grain on both ends of the Copper crepe. With the nonmetallic side facing out, wrap this piece around the main roll of the log and glue it in place, cutting away any excess bark.

   d. Use the soft brush to lightly dust the log with White pastel, brushing in the direction of the grain.

2. **Making the lichen**

   a. With the foam paintbrush, apply two coats of the Ivory paint to a 6 in/15 cm square of the Black crepe. The paint will pick up some of the pigment in the crepe and become more beige. If the crepe is still showing through, though, add another coat of paint.

   b. Cut the painted paper into 1 in/2.5 cm by 6 in/15 cm strips across the grain. Use template A to cut a scalloped edge along one of the long ends of each strip. When you've cut the edge of one section of the strip, you can lift the template and place it on the next section. Just keep a continuous strip as you lift and move the template. Gently stretch the edges and gently scissor curl them (see page 88) so the edges point down slightly.

SUPPLIES

Latte heavy crepe

Scissors

Metallic Copper extra-fine crepe

Aleene's Original Tacky Glue

Soft brush

PanPastel in Titanium White (100.5)

Foam paintbrush

Ivory acrylic paint

Mars Black heavy crepe

Bright Moss heavy crepe

Different shades of brown and beige paper

Templates (page 222)

c. Flip one of the strips over so the black side is facing up. Dot glue along the straight edge. Where you've dotted the glue, gather the paper by pushing together the little crinkles and holding them for a few seconds. This will make the paper start to curl. Form the strip into a small circle with the gathered paper at the center, pinching additional crinkles if necessary. Snip off any excess strip.

d. The remainder of the strip will be tucked under the lichen center. Dot the painted side of the strip with glue just along the straight edge. Glue it around the edge of the lichen center. When you've made it about 70 percent of the way around, snip the strip. Repeat, adding additional layers to the lichen until it's the size you prefer. You can make one huge patch of lichen or make a few clusters with their own centers and place them together as a little colony.

3. Making the moss

a. From the Bright Moss crepe, cut a strip across the grain 9 in/23 cm long and ¾ in/2 cm wide. Use template B to cut a scalloped edge on the strip. Once the whole strip is scalloped, cut a fringe across all the scallops. The trick is to keep each fringe cut ¼ in/6 mm deep from the point on the scallop you're cutting, rather than having each fringe a different height across the scallop. Twist the little fringes and then scissor curl them so they curve downward slightly.

b. Assemble the moss in the same way as the lichen. Once the moss edge is ready, gather the crinkles, create the center, and add additional layers, all in the same way.

4. For the leaves

a. From the brown and beige papers, cut 20 to 50 leaves, depending on how big a "forest floor you want for the log. Fold small rectangles of paper in half and freehand cut simple half-leaf shapes. Crumple and uncrumple them so they appear more natural. Arrange them beneath the log.

2b.

2c.

2d.

3a.

3b.

Rosy Bonnet & Amethyst Deceiver

SEE PAGE 23 AND 77, RESPECTIVELY

It was the gills that first drew me to these mushroom. I had noticed that the underside of honeycomb balls—party decorations made of tissue paper glued at intervals to create a honeycomb pattern—resembled the papery row of mushroom gills visible in flat-capped mushrooms. I found a miniature version of this paper and added crepe paper for the cap and paper straws to support the stems. I had to take some liberties with the design, because the smallest honeycomb paper I could find was still too large to re-create a rosy bonnet cap at its actual size of up to 2½ in/6.4 cm. For the even smaller amethyst deceiver, I had to scale up my paper mushrooms by 50 percent. But I have no qualms about my oversize mushrooms—I say, the more bonnet, the better! The rosy bonnet is pictured here; to make amethyst deceiver mushrooms, simply substitute different colors for the honeycomb paper pad and extra-heavy crepe (see the supplies list).

SUPPLIES

Scissors

Ivory extra-heavy crepe (for the amethyst deceiver, use Gold Heavy Crepe by Lia Griffin)

Aleene's Original Tacky Glue

Pad of Ivory honeycomb paper (for the amethyst deceiver, use Lilac)

Foam brush

Cosmetic wedge sponges

Paper straw

PanPastel in Permanent Red Tint (340.8) (for the rosy bonnet only)

Stem wire or toothpicks

Templates (pages 223-25)

OPTIONAL BASE

Cache pot

Floral foam

Freeze-dried moss

1. **Using the templates**

   a. The templates come in several sizes, grouped in sets of two. Each set has a cap template and a gills template. These templates are sized to work together in the same mushroom, so make sure not to mix cap and gill templates across sets.

2. **Making the cap**

   a. With template A2, cut a rectangle from the crepe, with the long side running across the grain. Fold the rectangle lengthwise along the dotted line on the template. The side of the rectangle where you can see the area that's been folded over will be the bottom of the cap. The opposite side will be the top. (For the amethyst deciever, fold your rectangle so that the metallic side of the crepe is inside of the fold.)

   b. Stretch the whole length of this fold almost all the way out, but don't stretch more than ½ in/12 mm down from the fold. To close this circle, open up the fold on one end of the circle and apply glue along the edge. Tuck the opposite side inside this opened fold, overlapping the two sides by about ¼ in/6 mm. Refold the glued edge, and press the seam with your fingers to set the glue.

   c. Cut a dime-size circle from the crepe.

2b., 2d.

3a., 3b.

3e.

4d., 4b., 4c.

4d.

5a.

d. With the bottom side of the cap facing up, dot the inner edge opposite the fold generously with glue. Gently gather the crepe paper from the edge of the cap toward the center. Use the dime-size circle to push the center of the cap flat.

e. Turn the cap top-side up. While the paper is still wet with glue, adjust the center of the cap. You can use your fingernails to pinch even pleats all the way around. Finally, dot glue in the little opening in the center of the cap, and pinch the hole closed.

f. For the amethyst deceiver, press the edges of the cap downward to make it convex and rounded on top. Hold the edges down for thirty seconds to help it keep its shape.

3. Making the gills

a. It takes two identical pieces of honeycomb paper to make a full ring of gills for the mushroom. Place template A1 on the honeycomb paper so the arrow on the template runs parallel with the little indentations that run up and down the honeycomb paper. Cut one template A1 section. To cut the second half of the gills, place template A1 on the honeycomb paper directly below the first template A1 you cut. This will ensure that the honeycomb pattern falls the same way on both halves of the gills, so they look even when you open them up.

b. Dot one of the two gill halves with glue, and then stack the other half on top. Allow to dry for a minute or so. Dot the top of this stack with glue, gently spread open the stack, and glue the bottom side of the stack to the top. Pinch along the edge to close. Let dry completely.

c. Open up the little three-dimensional honeycomb shape by gently pulling the outer edges away from one another.

d. Using a foam brush or a cosmetic sponge, brush glue over the entire bottom of the cap all the way out to the edge.

e. Lay the gills on the cap, stretching the honeycomb paper so the ends of the gills lie just inside the edge of the cap. As you stretch the paper, the hole in the center of the ring of honeycomb gills will open up, creating a port for the stem. You'll have a few minutes before the glue dries to adjust the honeycomb paper, so make sure the gills are evenly distributed along the cap edge. Working one section at a time, gently press the gills into the cap edge all the way around.

4. Building the stem

a. Use template F to cut a rectangle from the crepe. Fold the rectangle along the dotted line shown on the template. Stretch this fold as you stretched the fold to make the cap. Open the rectangle back up. Dot glue along one short edge of the stem rectangle, and place the paper straw on top of this line of glue.

b. Roll the rectangle around the straw tightly but without stretching the paper, making sure to align the ridge on the stem so it forms a complete ring. (You can exaggerate this ring by grasping the stem on either side of the ring and then pushing your hands together.)

c. Dot glue around the upper edge of the stem, then insert it into the space at the center of the honeycomb ring. Hold the stem in place for a minute to allow the glue to set.

d. For a rosy effect, use a wedge sponge to swipe the pink pastel from the middle of the cap outward, lifting before you reach the edge to create a gradient effect.

5. Styling

a. To create a cluster of mushrooms, use the different template sets included.

b. The paper straw at the center of the mushroom offers a lot of flexibility in styling. You can add mushrooms to a bouquet by inserting a piece of stem wire up the straw, giving it greater length. You can also fill a cache pot with floral foam topped with freeze-dried moss; just stick toothpicks into the foam and slip the straws over them.

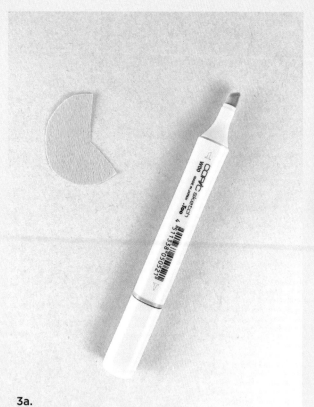

3a.

4a.

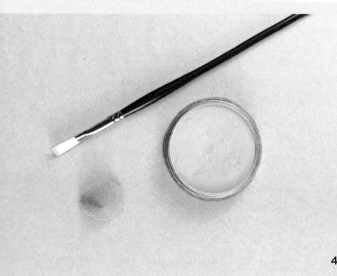

4b.

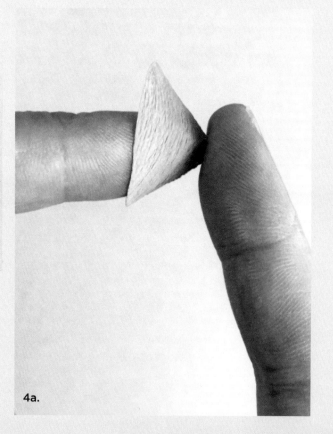

4a.

Bleeding Mycena

SEE PAGE 24

Though the individual mushrooms might seem unassuming as you make the first few, they come to life as the colony grows. When I'm assembling a cluster of mushrooms, I try to capture the quirky cohesiveness of live mycena colonies. So don't worry about the mushrooms being straight and equidistant. Let them clump here and there, and bend some of their little stems at odd angles.

1. **Making the caps**

   a. Because these funnel-shaped caps are built from paper that crinkles in just one direction, the caps will pull themselves out of form, creating strange little oblong shapes. Feel free to trim around the cap if it seems too lopsided, but in general, I think it's best to let them be a little bit quirky—it adds to the overall effect.

2. **Cutting the caps**

   a. I've included several sizes of the cap template to give the mushroom cluster variety. Choose one and use it to cut a cap from the doublette crepe. The arrow should be parallel with the grain of the crepe.

3. **Coloring the cap**

   a. The challenge in creating these mushrooms is that their color is a very subtle, brownish pink, rather than the bright, clear pinks usually available in doublette crepe. Additionally, the cap's color fades toward the edges. Color the cap as desired. I've used a beige gray Copic marker to color my whole cap, subduing the pink in the Honeysuckle/Coral doublette.

4. **Building the cap**

   a. With the colored side facing up, dot glue on the left side of the little wedge cut out of the bottom of the circle. Close the wedge by curving the cap into a funnel shape and pressing the right side of the wedge over the glued section on the left side. Hold this seam together for three seconds. Then, while the glue is still wet, round the cap by placing your finger into the tip of the funnel and gently pressing it into your hand or another finger. For the smaller caps, insert the small brush instead of your finger. If needed, trim the cap to make it a little bit more even.

   b. For lighter edges, use the small brush to apply the pastel in short, vertical strokes, all the way around the cap, then blend the edge where the pastel stops.

   c. For a slightly ruffled edge, gently stretch around the edge of the cap. You won't be able to stretch all the way around because of the way the grain falls on the cap, but even a little bit of frilling adds interest and personality.

SUPPLIES

Scissors

Doublette medium-weight crepe for the caps (I've used Honeysuckle/Coral)

Copic alcohol ink marker in Warm Gray (W1)

Aleene's Original Tacky Glue

Small paintbrush or makeup brush

PanPastel in Permanent Red Tint (340.8)

Eye protection

Wire snips

18-gauge cloth-covered stem wire

Aubergine extra-fine crepe, to cover the stems

Templates (page 225)

OPTIONAL BASE

2¾ in/7 cm polystyrene half ball for base

Freeze-dried moss, a variety of light brown paper for dead leaves, or Bright Moss heavy crepe to cover base

Olive green thread

OPTIONAL "BLOOD"

Red glue stick

Hot glue gun

Wax paper

d. To create a cluster of mushrooms, make several caps using a mix of the cap templates included.

5. Making the stems

a. Using eye protection and wire snips, cut a stem for each cap. For a single mushroom, 2 in/5 cm is a nice stem length. For a mushroom cluster, you'll want several lengths of cloth-covered stem wire, ranging from 2 to 3½ in/5 to 9 cm.

b. Using the instructions on page 92, cut several stem strips, and wrap the stems in Aubergine crepe.

c. Dot the tip of the stem with glue and gently press it into the underside of the mushroom cap. Repeat for each additional cap until every mushroom has a stem.

d. The part of the mushroom cap with the seam is the rear of the cap for display purposes; the seams should all face the same direction. Once the glue is dry, gently bend the stems, allowing them to lean away from the center of the wire cluster. For mushrooms that are growing out of the side of something, bend all the wires up about 45 degrees from the wrapped bottoms of the wires.

6. Styling

a. To add moss, hold clumps of freeze-dried moss against the foam shape, and secure it by wrapping it with the olive thread. Repeat until the entire foam shape is covered. Clip the thread, leaving 5 in/12.5 cm of thread at the end, and tie this end tightly to the other end of the thread to form a knot. Clip excess thread. Push the wrapped bottom 1 in/2.5 cm of the stem wires into the middle of the half ball. You can cover this half ball with freeze-dried moss, "dead leaves," or "moss."

b. Add the mushrooms, pushing the bottom 1 in/2.5 cm of the stem wires into the foam.

c. To add "blood" to the stem of a mushroom, load the red glue stick into the glue gun and dot a few drops on the bottom of the stem. For full-on oozing, lay the mushroom on wax paper, and apply drops from the bottom of the stem and down onto the wax paper. When the glue cools, peel off the wax paper.

5c.

6a.

Calypso Orchid

SEE PAGE 27

Calypso orchids trick insects into pollinating multiple flowers, despite offering them no nectar, with little variations that thwart insect attempts to identify and avoid the deceptive flower. So don't stress about creating an exact copy for this project—variation makes them more realistic.

SEE PAGE 27

SUPPLIES

Tsukineko Memento Dew Drop dye ink pad in Rhubarb Stalk

White doublette crepe

Scissors

1 standard-size marble

Copic marker in Aubergine (V99)

Any yellow water-based marker or highlighter

Eye protection

Wire snips

18-gauge cloth-covered stem wire

Aleene's Original Tacky Glue

Design Master Colortool spray paint in Lavender (708)

Linen extra-fine crepe

¼ in/6 mm dowel

Juniper extra-fine crepe

Deep Olive/Olive Green doublette crepe

Templates (page 226)

OPTIONAL BASE

Pot

Floral foam

Freeze-dried moss

1. **Making the labellum**

   a. Use the ink pad to paint a 2-in-/5-cm-thick stripe across the grain of the White doublette. This stripe has to be just wide enough to accommodate one template A piece, but you can make it wider if you plan to make more orchids. Lift at the bottom of every stroke to create a soft edge. The ink pad applies color to the raised ridges in the crepe paper, which will mimic the striping on the orchid's purse. Position template A on the stripe so the bottom half of the template has color but the top doesn't. Following the instructions on page 87, cut one template A labellum petal on the fold for each orchid you'd like to make.

   b. Place the marble in the middle of the back half of the labellum and stretch both sides around the marble to create a little pouch. Using the instructions on page 88, scissor curl the rounded top edge of the labellum.

   c. Using the Copic marker, dot the rounded area around the top of the labellum with little speckles, following the speckling directions on page 98. Use the yellow marker to very gently apply a dot to the area just in front of the purse and behind the speckles. The yellow area should be about ⅛ in/3 mm wide.

   d. Using eye protection and wire snips, cut a 9 in/23 cm length of stem wire. Cut a 2 in/5 cm stem strip of the White doublette and wrap the tip of the wire. Dot the area below the glue line of the labellum with glue and wrap it around the wrapped tip so the tip of the wire stem hits about where the glue line on the template falls.

2. **Making the other petals**

   a. Using the directions on page 99, spray stripes of the Lavender paint onto the Linen extra-fine crepe. Space the stripes so they're longer than the D template. Cut two template C petals on the fold, positioning the template on the strip so the part of the strip that has a lighter coat of paint makes up the bottom half or third of the petal. Repeat to cut three template D sepals and one hood petal from template B.

   b. Stretch the B piece, the hood, into a big, gentle cup (see page 88). (Make sure you're stretching only the area above the

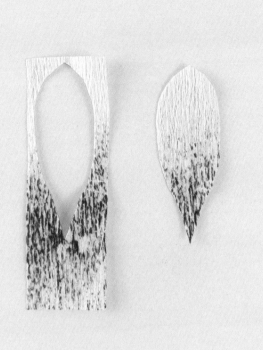

1a.

1b.

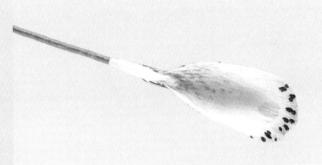

1c.

2b.

2d.

3b.

3c.

glue line indicated on the template.) Dot the area under the glue line with glue and attach it to the stem wire, opposite the labellum. Bend the wire below the petals to form a 90-degree angle.

c. Give each of the C and D petals some personality by stretching the edges a little bit, lightly scissor curling, or gently twisting the petals. The effect should be subtle.

d. Attach the C petals on either side of the hood. Attach one of the D sepals in the space between the two C petals, one to the right of the C petal on the right side of the flower, and one to the left of the C petal on the left side.

3. **Finishing the flower**

    a. With the ¼ in/6 mm dowel, very gently curl back the petals so they stand up over the labellum.

    b. Using the instructions on page 92, cut stem strips from Juniper extra-fine crepe and wrap the first 3 in/7.5 cm of the stem. Cut a template E spathe on the fold from the darker part of the Lavender-sprayed strip. Dot glue at the bottom of the spathe, and glue it around the stem ½ in/12 mm from the back of the flower, so it points upward. Continue to wrap the stem with stem strips, wrapping over the bottom ¼ in/6 mm of the spathe. Wrap to the bottom of the wire.

    c. Using template F, cut one leaf on the fold from the Olive Green doublette. Fold the leaf in half vertically to create a crease, then open it up, and very gently scissor curl all the way around the leaf. Dot it with glue below the glue line, and attach it to the stem 1½ in/4 cm from the bottom end of the stem.

    d. If you'd like to display the orchid in a pot, put a piece of floral foam in the pot so it's firmly lodged in place, cover the top with freeze-dried moss, and stick the bottom of the wire into the foam.

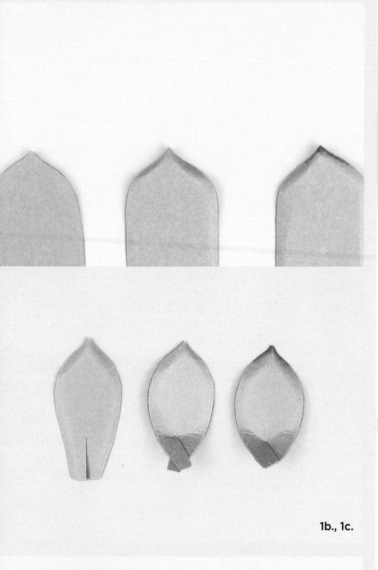

2c.

1b., 1c.

2a.

3a., 3b., 3c.

Echeveria

SEE PAGE 31

This was the first project I started building for this book. Exuberant and terrified, I spent a week working out color combinations for a fabulous multicolored, multi-succulent display. Moving past the conviction that it must be beautiful, perfect, and abundant, and coming to grips with the fact that this was a finite project with deadlines to keep in mind, was an important step for me and helped me keep my ambitions in check as I tackled additional projects. But I still have wistful feelings about those olive green, pink, purple, and turquoise succulents in my mind's eye. I hope this project will inspire you to make your own many-colored succulent garden!

1. **Preparing the center leaves**

   a. Follow the instructions on page 96 to add a wash of acrylic paint, using a solution of 1 part craft paint with 2 parts water. Because the consistency of acrylic paint can differ from brand to brand, I recommend doing a patch test to make sure you like the opacity. Paint one sheet each of all six colors of cardstock, making sure to apply the paint on the smoothest side of the cardstock. The paper will buckle and curl after you've painted it, but that's nothing to worry about.

   b. When cutting leaves, make sure any brush lines on the cardstock run up and down the template, rather than side to side. For the center, use templates A, B, and C to cut one of each template from the Purple Palisades cardstock. For row 2, cut five template D leaves from the Purple Palisades cardstock. You'll borrow one of these template D leaves to finish the center. For row 3, cut five template E leaves from the Turquoise Mist cardstock. For row 4, cut six template F leaves from the Robin cardstock. For row 5, cut seven template F leaves from the Navajo cardstock. For row 6, cut eight template G leaves from the Pearlescent Turquoise cardstock. For row 7, cut eight template H leaves from the Light Green cardstock.

   c. Emboss all forty-two leaves, placing the cardstock on the foam sheet and following the instructions on page 96 for embossing cardstock leaf edges and points. Next, use the PanPastel and wedge sponge to color the tips of each leaf as shown. Now, further shape the first three leaves. Note the slit line down the middle of the bottom part of templates A, B, and C. Cut along this slit line on the A leaf. Dot the flap on the right side of the slit with glue. Move the left flap sideways to overlap the right, about where the line on the template radiates to the lower right. Hold the overlapped flaps in place for a few seconds to let the glue set. Trim the bottom of the leaf

SUPPLIES

DecoArt Americana Wisteria acrylic craft paint

Paintbrush

Scissors

Bazzill Purple Palisades cardstock (300907)

Bazzill Turquoise Mist cardstock (301089)

Darice Robin cardstock (GX-CF-30R)

Bazzill Navajo cardstock (301077)

Darice Pearlescent Turquoise cardstock (GX-GEM310)

Canson Mi-tientes in Light Green

Embossing tools, ¼ in/6 mm and ¹⁄₁₆ in/2 mm

PanPastel in Magenta (80740)

Cosmetic wedge sponge

Foam sheet, ⅛ in/3 mm thick

Aleene's Original Tacky Glue

Colortool spray paint in Basil (676)

Ivory extra-heavy crepe

Gold/Orange doublette crepe

Eye protection

Wire snips

18-gauge cloth-covered stem wire

Packing tape

Templates (page 226)

by cutting as indicated by the curved lines drawn toward the bottom of the template. Repeat for all remaining leaves, but only trim the bottom leaves of A through C.

2. Building the succulent components

a. Now you're going to set your first four leaves at 90-degree angles to each other, forming a kind of square. The template A leaf will sit on the template B leaf's lap, at a 90-degree angle to template A. The B leaf will sit on the C leaf's lap, with C opposite B. The C leaf will sit in the D leaf's lap, with D opposite A. When attaching the first three leaves, bend the base of the template forward toward the front of the leaf and dot the underside of the bent front edge with glue before attaching it to the next leaf.

b. With the center complete, all subsequent leaves will be attached in rings.

c. Using a bit more glue than usual, glue two D leaves together, setting the bottom of one leaf on the "lap" of another, so they overlap about 50 percent. Set the leaves so they form a 90-degree angle. (This angle will decrease with each subsequent row.) Repeat, adding two additional leaves. Each new leaf is added on the left and should overlap the preceding leaves in a given row. When you've gone all the way around a row, dot the bottom of the last leaf with glue and glue it to the top of the first leaf.

d. As you work outward, adding additional rows, overlap the bottoms of the leaves less, and place the rounded upper edge of each petal—I think of them as shoulders—closer together. For each row, decrease both the overlap and the space between the leaf "shoulders" by about 10 percent. Use extra glue when you build the rows so that if they make a misshapen circle, you can adjust the leaf placement a bit. But don't feel like you need to make a perfect circle for each row. Wonky rows will create a more realistic succulent.

e. Assemble all remaining rows in the same way.

3. Making the flower spike

a. Following the instructions on page 99 for working with spray paint, spray an 8 by 8 in/20 by 20 cm square of the Ivory crepe with the Basil paint. From this square, cut two or three stem strips. Stretch out a section of the spray-painted crepe and use template I to cut six bracts on the fold (see page 87).

Cup the whole inside of the bracts, following the instructions on page 88.

b. Cut four template J pieces from the Gold/Orange doublette. Curl the tips of the petals away from the gold side. Dot the bottom of the gold side with glue and twist the bottom to close up the flower.

c. Following the instructions on page 92 for wrapping wire, wrap the top ¼ in/6 mm of the wire with the crepe. Dot a bract below the glue line and glue it onto the wire so the glue line falls at the line on the wire where the wrapping stops. Resume wrapping, starting by wrapping over the glue line on the bract. Repeat this process to add another bract. Repeat again as if for a third bract, except this time, you'll put one of the flowers where the bract should be, positioning the flower's glue line where the bract's glue line would be. Position a bract over the flower so the flower petals just barely peek out. Glue and wrap for ½ in/12 mm and repeat. This time the bract should cover less of the flower. Repeat twice more, wrapping ½ in/12 mm farther each time. This time, the bract should be lifted up to let most of the flower show. Use the tip of a wire to help arrange the petals so they look natural under the lifted bract. Wrap down to the end of the stem. Curve the top portion of wine to form a hook-like shape. Decide how tall you want the flower spike, then bend the wire at the point that would be the bottom. Snip the wire 2½ in/6 cm below the bend.

4. Assembling the succulent

a. You'll attach the parts of the succulent together by gluing the bottoms of each row and stacking the tab sections. Try to position each row so the leaves are somewhat staggered. Because these rows have different numbers of leaves, you won't be able to do it perfectly, but try to avoid having a leaf directly behind a leaf in front of it.

b. The last two rows are easier to stagger, since you can just position the leaves in a given row in the spaces between the leaves in an adjacent row. Before you glue on the very last row, use the packing tape to secure the bottom section of the wire (the section below the bend) to the bottom of the second-to-last row. Then glue on the final row.

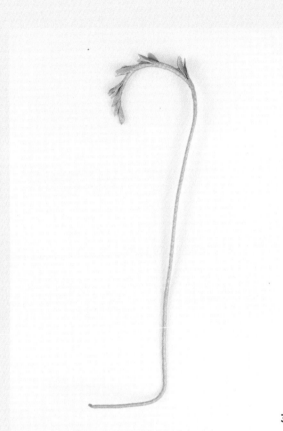

3c.

4a.

4b.

Blue Torch Cactus

SEE PAGE 32

This cactus is a lovely example of one of the extremely neat things you can do with crepe paper. You'll bend and stretch the crepe to sculpt the cactus into ribs that round at the top. A metallic fringe will stand in for stamens.

It would be tragic to stop at blue for these—if you have the materials, I'd suggest making them in pink, blue, violet, white, and gold for a lovely, whimsical effect.

SUPPLIES

Deep Olive/Olive Green doublette crepe (2 folds)

Scissors

Light-colored colored pencil

Aleene's Original Tacky Glue

Ruler

Krylon Outdoor Décor satin paint in Rainwater

Mask (optional)

Tissue paper that's a semi-metallic gold on one or both sides

White/Vanilla doublette crepe

18-gauge cloth-covered stem wire

Pineapple heavy crepe

Soft brush

PanPastel in Permanent Red (340.3)

PanPastel in Bright Yellow Green (680.3)

Floral tape

Juniper extra-fine crepe (optional)

Awl

Templates (page 227)

1. **Making the cactus**

   a. Decide how tall you want the cactus, and cut the doublette crepe with the grain to a length that matches your desired height. Cut the second fold to match. Using the colored pencil, draw a line 1 in/2.5 cm from the long edge of one of the lengths of green crepe. Working 8 to 10 in/20 to 25 cm at a time, dot the area between the pencil line and the edge with glue. Line up the two long ends of the lengths of crepe, and overlap the long edge of the second length so that it meets the pencil line on the first length. Press to help set the glue. Repeat until the two pieces are glued together, overlapped by 1 in/2.5 cm.

   b. With a ruler, draw a line parallel to the overlapping edge, 1 in/2.5 cm over. Repeat, drawing a line parallel to the line you just drew. Repeat until you're 1 in/2.5 cm from the other long edge of the crepe paper. Draw a line on the other side of the overlapped edge, and repeat until you've reached 1 in/2.5 cm from the opposite long edge. Accordion fold the whole piece of crepe along these lines.

2. **Shaping the top of the cactus**

   a. Lay out the accordion-folded crepe, with the lighter side up. At one of the short ends, grasp two of the mountain folds together and stretch them out along the fold. Stretch the top 3 in/7.5 cm of these two folds until their upper edge faces almost 90 degrees back from where it was facing before you stretched it. Repeat for the rest of the mountain folds along this short end.

3. **Assembling the cactus**

   a. To prepare the body of the cactus, trim the excess ½ in/12 mm of crepe paper on either side of the accordian-folded piece.

   b. To close the cactus, start at the edge that ends in a half mountain fold. Apply glue under the half mountain fold and under the full mountain fold next to it for the entire length of the cactus. Form the cactus into a cylinder by tucking the full mountain fold on the opposite edge underneath the full mountain fold that is covered in glue. Press the half mountain fold against the first half of the next mountain fold. Allow to dry.

1b.

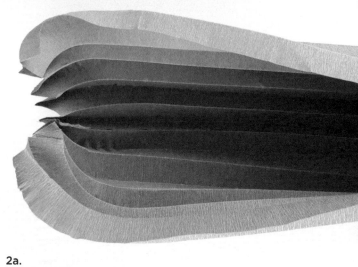

2a.

4a.

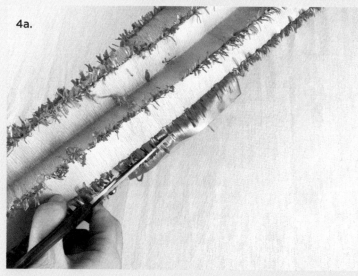

4a.

3b.

c. To join the upper ribs of the cactus, glue what was the short edge of the crepe paper together in sections, working one fold at a time. Dot glue at the very top edge of one side of a fold, and pinch the fold together with the next one to glue them closed. Repeat, gluing together pairs of ribs with glue all the way around the cactus. Next, dot what was the top edge of one pair of ribs with glue and attach it to the same spot on the fold on the opposite side of the circle. Dot glue along the edge of one of the remaining pairs of ribs, and glue it to the line where the first two sets of ribs meet. Repeat with the remaining set of ribs.

d. Stand the cactus up and spray it with the Rainwater spray paint. (It's best to spray this outside; consider wearing a mask.) Let it dry, then add a second coat. If needed, add a third and even a fourth coat. Lighter coats are better for the crepe paper than heavy ones. Allow to dry completely.

4. Adding the spines

a. Cut a 2 by 6 in/5 by 15 cm strip of the gold tissue paper. Fold it in half lengthwise, and snip a fringe all the way across the folded edge. The fringe should reach three-quarters of the way from the fold out to the edge of the tissue paper. Starting at the bottom of the cactus, apply a very thin line of glue to one of the ribs, working in 6 in/15 cm increments. Open up the folded fringed tissue. Place it on the glue so the crease running down the middle of all the fringes is directly on top of the glue. Repeat until you've covered the whole rib. Once the glue is dry, pinch the two halves of the strip of fringes forward to once again fold the fringes lengthwise but in the opposite direction. Trim the fringes to roughly ½ in/12 mm long, cutting away the outer edge that was holding the fringes together. Repeat for the remaining ribs.

5. Making the flowers

a. Cut a 6 in/15 cm White doublette stem strip. Wrap the top 1 in/2.5 cm of the stem wire three times with the doublette. Cut a 6 in/15 cm strip of the Pineapple crepe to wrap the wire, starting from ½ in/12 mm below the tip of the wire, overlapping the doublette and spiraling down the wire until you run out of strip.

b. Cut a template A piece from the Pineapple crepe. Follow the instructions on page 92 for making confetti-style stamens.

c. Once the stamens are dry, dot the area below the glue line (as indicated on the template) with glue. Place the stem wire on one end of the stamen piece,

making sure that the wire tip extends 1 in/2.5 cm beyond the tips of the fringes. Press the wire down into the glued area of the stamens and then loosely roll the stamens around the wire.

d. Angle the top part of the wire downward so it seems to rest on the bottom section of the fringe. Push the fringe out and away from the wire all the way around. Working in sections, flatten the fringe together in your hands and finger curl the fringe toward the center.

e. Cut ten petals on the fold (see page 87) from the White doublette crepe, using template B. With scissors, curl the petal back, following the instructions on page 88. Apply these petals evenly around the fringes, matching up the glue line on the templates with the spot on the fringe that's wrapped around the wire. The Vanilla side of these petals should face the center.

f. Cut ten petals from the White doublette crepe using template C. With the soft brush, dust a small amount of the red pastel from the tips of the petals to about halfway down the petal, lifting at the end of your stroke so the color fades evenly. Repeat with the green pastel over the top of the red. Scissor curl these petals even more dramatically than the B petals. Attach the C petals just as you did the B petals, staggering the C petals between the B petals.

g. Wrap the bottom of the flower tightly with floral tape, stretching as you wrap to activate the adhesive. If you like the finish of the floral tape, feel free to leave it. Otherwise, cover it with some Juniper extra-fine crepe.

6. Attaching the flowers

a. Very carefully use the awl to poke a hole in the spot where you'd like to place the flower. Angle the flower and fleshy stem so they meet the rest of the wire at about a 45-degree angle. Insert the wire into the cactus and, just before you push it all the way in, dot a very small amount of glue around the base of the fleshy part of the stem. Hold it in place for a moment to allow the glue to set. Repeat with your preferred number of flowers.

b. The cactus will stand up on its own, but for extra security, you can use a cylinder-shaped container weighted down with gravel, marbles, dried beans, or the like. (An empty Pringles can would be great for this.) Just slip the bottom of the cactus over the container.

5f.

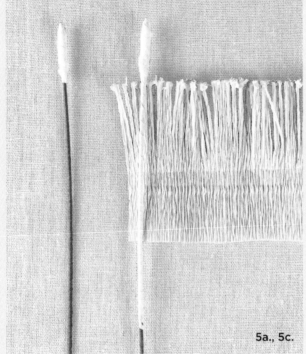

5a., 5c.

5d.

1a.

1b.

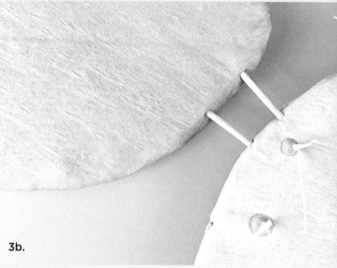

3b.

4a.

2c.

Prickly Pear Cactus

SEE PAGE 35

Between wrapping the cactus paddles in floral tape and covering the cactus in little spines, this project is an exercise in patience. Fortunately, to make it easier to handle without damaging the paper thorns, the cactus is one-sided, with the reverse side blank. (You'll be glad when you're finally adding spines to that last little paddle!)

1. **Making the paddle base**

    a. Use template A to cut a paddle from the foam sheet. Cut two layers of tissue paper 4 in/10 cm wide and long enough to reach from the paddle base on one side over the paddle and to the paddle base on the other side. Gently twist it into a loose rope. The next step can get a little messy, so wear gloves if you don't want glue all over your hands. Starting from one end of the rope and working 4 to 6 in/10 to 15 cm at a time, dot one side of the rope with glue. Starting at one side of the base of the foam sheet paddle, glue the rope along the edge of the paddle until you reach the other side of the base. Trim off the excess rope.

    b. Dot the first 2 in/5 cm of floral tape with glue. Attach the glued section to the middle of the paddle and begin to wrap around the paddle with the floral tape, stretching as you wrap to make a smooth surface. Make sure that you're tightly wrapping the edges, which should compress when you pull the floral tape taut. It's fine if the floral tape you've already wrapped lifts off the surface of the foam as you work. When you've wrapped the whole surface, cut the tape and dot the last 2 in/5 cm with glue. Wrap this last glued portion onto the paddle. Press for a minute to set the glue.

2. **Covering the paddles**

    a. Lay out the Moss crepe and cut a rectangle 3 in/7.5 cm taller than the paddle and 1 in/2.5 cm narrower than the paddle. Stretch out most of the crinkles.

    b. Using the wedge sponge, spread tacky glue over the entire surface of one side of the foam paddle. Stretch the Moss crepe over the paddle, pulling it so tight that all the crinkles smooth out. Press the crepe against the middle of the paddle and smooth it over the surface out toward the edges.

    c. Trim the paper around the paddle. On the curved parts of the paddle, cut a ¼ by ¼ in/6 by 6 mm fringe in the Moss crepe paddle cover. Sponge tacky glue onto the paddle and the lower edge of the Moss crepe fringe. Smooth the fringed edge of the paddle cover over the edge of the paddle. Repeat to cover the reverse side.

    d. Repeat for the remaining paddle, using the B template.

SUPPLIES

Scissors

Extra-thick foam sheet, ¼ in/6 mm thick

Tissue paper in any color

Aleene's Original Tacky Glue

Floral tape

Moss extra-heavy crepe

Cosmetic wedge sponge

Awl

Toothpicks

Needle-nose pliers

Soft brush

PanPastel in Permanent Green Tint (640.8)

Foam or papier-mâché eggs in assorted sizes, approximately 1½ to 2 in/4 to 5 cm tall

Cyclamen heavy crepe

Azalea heavy crepe

PanPastel in Permanent Red (340.5)

Off-white cardstock

Art-C Ultra Chalk Soft Matte Paint in Sand

Floral foam

Fairly heavy planting pot

Freeze-dried moss

Dowel (optional)

Templates (page 229)

3. Attaching the paddles

a. You'll attach the second paddle to the upper right side of the first paddle as shown. Make sure to pick a spot where the bottom of the second paddle makes contact with a ¾ in/2 cm section of the first paddle.

b. Very carefully use the awl to poke a 1½ in/4 cm deep hole on either end of the section where the two paddles will make contact, making sure the holes are ¼ in/6 mm in from either edge. Poke two corresponding 1½ in/4 cm holes on the base of the smaller paddle where it will make contact with the larger paddle. Dot one half of a toothpick with glue and insert it into one of the large paddle holes so half of the toothpick sticks out. Repeat for the next hole on the bigger paddle. Then dot the two exposed toothpicks with glue, and, using the needle-nose pliers to grip the toothpicks, push them into the smaller paddle. When the space between the two paddles is too small to use the pliers, use your hands to gently push the two paddles together.

c. Use this same method to insert two toothpicks halfway into either side of the base of the cactus.

4. Adding color to the cactus

a. Use the soft brush to apply the Green pastel over the surface of the paddles. Apply more to the middle of the paddles, allowing more Moss color to show through at the edges.

5. Making the pears

a. Press the large end of a foam egg onto a hard, flat surface so it flattens out, but stays rounded around the edges of the flattened section.

b. Lay out the Cyclamen crepe and cut a rectangle 4 in/10 cm wide and 1 in/2.5 cm taller than the egg. Place the egg in the middle of the crepe, parallel to the grain. Following the instructions on page 89, stretch the paper around the egg and glue it closed. Cut a 4 in/10 cm square from the Azalea crepe and stretch it almost all the way out. Cut some rough circles from the Azalea crepe that are just big enough to cover the flattened section and glue them in place. With your thumb, press all along the inside of this circle to crush the foam underneath and make the pear cap seem indented. If the foam won't budge, don't worry about it!

c. Use the soft brush to apply the Red pastel to the lower half or to one side of the pear. (It looks

especially nice to apply the color to different areas of each pear.) Repeat, using a variety of egg sizes, if possible, and then attach the pears the same way you attached the paddles, using only one toothpick this time.

6. Making the spines

a. From the cardstock, cut long (as spines go), very skinny rectangles, ½ to 1 in/12 mm to 2.5 cm long.

b. To prepare the cactus, use the sand-colored matte paint to apply spine cushions. Dot the paddle with small beads of the matte paint. The dots don't have to be in a perfect pattern, but I shoot for a general hexagon pattern. In other words, if you can imagine a hexagon pattern with a spine at every point and one right in the middle, that should give you a sense of the way they're distributed. It's also completely fine to just do rows that are staggered by 50 percent. I like to space the spines 1 in/2.5 cm apart, but adjust to your liking. As you move on to the smaller paddle, use the same pattern but place them a little closer together.

c. Once the spine cushions are dry, dot one with a small bead of tacky glue and stick two spines so they stand up in the glue drop. Repeat, covering one side and the edges with spines. (Don't try to do this in one continuous session—you'll want to take breaks!)

7. Styling

a. To display the cactus, choose a foam shape that's big enough to wedge firmly into the pot and sit about 1 in/2.5 cm below the rim.

b. Stick the cactus toothpicks into the foam at the center of the pot. Cover the area around the cactus with the freeze-dried moss to hide the foam. If your cactus needs additional support, insert a dowel into the floral foam so that half of it sticks up out of the foam in the pot. Tape the dowel to the back of the lower paddle. Leave it like this, or cover the taped dowel by gluing a strip of Moss crepe over it.

5b.

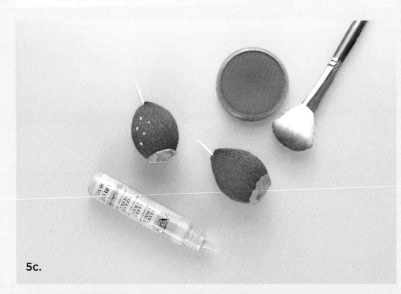

5c.

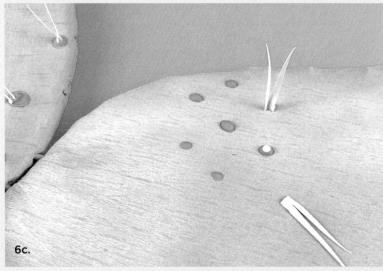

6c.

Night-Blooming Cereus

SEE PAGE 36

Given how rarely we get the opportunity to see a live cereus bloom, I'm excited to share this ever-blooming version. I hope someday to design a paper nectar bat so my cereus will have a pollinator!

1. **Making the flower's center**

    a. Using template A, cut a fringe piece from the Pineapple crepe, and fringe across the top of the template. Dot glue on the fringe piece below where the glue line on the template inidcates, and wrap the fringe piece around the tip of a full stem wire. (The tip of the wire should not be visible.) Cut a stem strip from the Eggnog heavy crepe and wrap it around 5 in/12 cm of wire. Press each little fringe down so it forms a 90-degree angle with the wire. When you've gone all the way around, the fringes should radiate like a star from the wire.

    b. Cut a template B shape from the cardstock. Using template C, cut two stamen pieces from the Eggnog heavy crepe. Use the wedge sponge to smear glue on the cardstock piece, and place it on top of one stamen piece so the two bottom edges align and the cardstock piece is centered along this edge. Smear the front of the cardstock piece and the second stamen piece with glue, and lay the second stamen piece on top. Apply gentle pressure to help the glue set.

    c. Fringe up to the glue line/cardstock edge. Dot glue on the inner edge of one side of the stamens below the glue line/cardstock edge. Glue it to the opposite edge, closing up the funnel. Following the instructions on page 92 for confetti stamens, add Pineapple crepe pollen to the Eggnog stamens.

    d. When the glue is completely dry, gather two-thirds of the stamens to one side of the center. Finger curl them all up and toward the center. Thread the stem wire through the funnel until the tip extends 1 in/2.5 cm beyond the stamens. Use the floral tape to secure the funnel to the wire.

2. **Adding petals**

    a. From the White/Vanilla doublette, cut eight template D petals on the fold (see page 87). Following the instructions on page 88, gently cup the whole inside of each petal just a bit, leaving the edges unstretched. Dot glue on the White side of a petal below where the glue line on the template indicates, and line the petal up with the glue line on the stamens. Add three more so the four petals are distributed evenly around the center like compass points. The next four petals go in the spaces between the first four.

    b. Repeat this process, adding eight petals from template E and then eight from template F.

SUPPLIES

Scissors

Pineapple heavy crepe

18-gauge cloth-covered stem wire

Aleene's Original Tacky Glue

Eggnog heavy crepe

White cardstock

Cosmetic wedge sponge

Floral tape of any color

White/Vanilla doublette crepe

Design Master Tint IT spray paint in Sepia (538)

Raspberry extra-fine crepe

Deep Olive/Olive Green doublette crepe

Elmer's Multi-Purpose Spray Adhesive

Templates (page 230)

1b., 1c.

1a.

1d.

2a.

2b.

c. To prepare the White/Vanilla doublette for your last two rows, spray paint across the top and bottom of an 18 in/45.5 cm length of the doublette. The last two rows of petals use a total of sixteen template G petals from the spray-painted crepe.

d. Repeat to make a second flower.

3. **Wrapping the stem**

   a. Following the instructions on page 92, cut the stem strips from the Raspberry crepe, and wrap the stem from the back of the flower down to the bottom of the stem.

4. **Making the leaves**

   a. Cereus flowers grow out of the sides of long leaves. These leaves have a thick vein running down the middle that curves off to one side and becomes the stem of a flower. Leaving 3 in/7.5 cm of the upper part of the stem to grow out of the side of the leaf, bend the wire so that it curves gently to one side as pictured. Cut two template H leaf pieces, one with the Deep Olive facing up and one with the Olive Green facing up. Place one H leaf piece, Deep Olive–side up and use the wedge sponge to apply a thin coat of spray adhesive all over the leaf. Place the bent wire down the middle of the leaf so that the flower stem exits the leaf 1 to 2 in/1.5 to 5 cm from the tip of the leaf. Press the second H leaf piece onto the first leaf piece, creating a sandwich with a wire inside. Repeat for the second flower, using the second leaf template.

   b. When the two stems are finished, wrap them together with the Raspberry stem strips from 1 in/2.5 cm below each leaf to the bottom. Bend the overall stem into an arch. Bend the short flower stems at a rounded 45-degree angle, so it faces up.

2c.

4b.

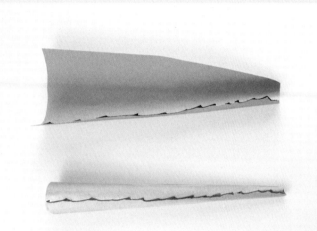

2b.

1a., 1b.

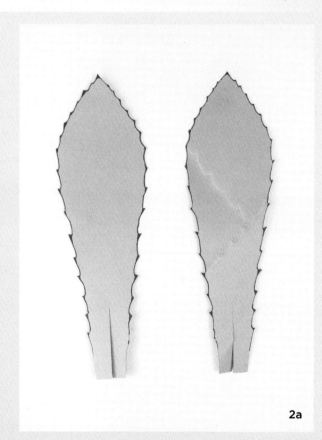

2c.

2a

Agave

SEE PAGE 39

My favorite part of this project (and of agaves in general) is the spiny pattern indented on the surface of each leaf. There is almost certainly some complex and mysterious geometry that dictates the placement of these lines. Since I haven't decoded it yet, I prefer to place the lines somewhat at random. If you crack the code, let me know! Otherwise, I recommend faking it when you show off your agave—if anyone catches you out, make sure they send me their secret formula.

1. Building the center

a. Use template A to cut an inner cone piece from the Green paper. Color the curved edge of the piece and the fronts of the "thorns" with the Peony marker. Use the wedge sponge to swipe Violet pastel onto one side of the paper. With the A piece parallel to the dowel, bend the paper around the dowel and roll it down the paper, which will make it easier to roll up smoothly.

b. Roll the piece up into a cone (with the color on the outside). Start by rolling the upper, curvy edge sideways and downward at the same time, then bring the rest of the curvy edge down and around. When the top of the cone has rolled into a point and the curvy edge has completely covered the straight edge, dot under the curvy edge with hot glue, and glue the cone shut. Use scissors to round off the very tip of the cone.

2. Preparing the leaves

a. Use template B to cut 15 leaves from the Green paper. Color the edges just as you did for the cone, except that you'll do both sides. Follow the instructions on page 95 for embossing a pattern. Place the paper on the foam sheet and use the smaller embossing tool to make spiny leaf edge lines across the leaves. These lines can originate on either side of the leaf and run to the opposite edge. You might also add lines that begin at a point on the first line and continue upward at an angle. Or you can follow the suggested lines on template B. Once you've embossed the pattern with the small tool, you can use the larger tool to emboss alongside one side of the embossed lines, which will help make the indentation feel more three-dimensional.

b. Just as you did for the cone piece, sweep Violet pastel over each side of the leaf. Use the dowel to curl the upper edges of each leaf somewhat downward and toward the center (see instructions for curling, page 88). Bend the sides of the leaf toward the center so the leaf is rounded.

SUPPLIES

Scissors

Canson Mi-Teintes Light Green paper (#480)

Copic marker in Peony (RV69)

Cosmetic wedge sponge

PanPastel in Violet Tint (470.8)

½ in/12 mm dowel

Hot glue gun

Embossing tools, ¼ in/6 mm and $\frac{1}{16}$ in/2 mm

Extra-thick foam sheet, ¼ in/6 mm thick

Aleene's Original Tacky Glue

Templates (pages 231–33)

3a.

4a., 4b.

c. At the bottom of template B is a slit line and two lines that run from the slit in a diagonal line toward the lower right. Cut a corresponding slit in the leaves. Dot tacky glue on the right tab, between the slit and the diagonal line. Using the template as a visual guide, bring the left-hand tab over the right, lining up the slit side of the left tab with the uppermost diagonal line on the right. Repeat to prep four additional leaves for row 1.

d. Repeat to prepare leaves for row 2, which will have five leaves. For this row, glue the left tab over the right, lining up the slit side of the tab with the second diagonal line from the top. For row 3, use template C to prepare five leaves.

3. Building the rings

a. To build the first ring, dot a heavier than normal amount of glue on one of the B leaves at the underside of the leaf, where the tabs overlap. Place this glued section on top of the same section on another B leaf, positioning the leaves at a seventy-degree angle to each other. (No need to get the leaf spacing exactly right: the extra glue will allow for some adjustment once the ring is complete.) Repeat to add the remaining three leaves. Adjust if necessary.

b. Repeat to make two more ring's of template B leaves, and one ring of template C leaves.

4. Assembling the agave

a. Glue the rings of leaves to each other. As much as possible, try to keep the leaves in one row offset from the leaves in the rows on either side (in other words, it's better not to have a leaf directly in front of or behind another leaf, although a little bit of that is fine). Before you add the last row, use the dowel to curl it backward as shown. These are the older leaves of the agave that have started to droop back toward the ground.

b. Trim the base of the cone so it's completely flat. Dot the bottom edge with tacky glue and place it in the center of the stack of rings. Hold in place for ten seconds and then leave to dry. If the tacky glue isn't sticking, use the hot glue gun.

Star Cactus

SEE PAGE 40

I've taken a lot of liberties with this design, making the paper version larger and rounder than it is in nature, to make this a more accessible project. I hope that knowing it isn't a perfect replica will help you feel at perfect liberty to add your own variations. I'd love to see a collection of these in other colors of crepe and spangled with more dramatically colored pom-poms.

SUPPLIES

Drawing compass

5.8 in/14.8 cm Styrofoam ball

Floral foam knife

Scissors

Two 12 by 8 in/30.5 by 20 cm foam sheets, $\frac{1}{16}$ in/2 mm thick

Fern/Moss doublette crepe

Cosmetic wedge sponge

Aleene's Original Tacky Glue

Sewing pins

Hampton Art Chalk Marker (fine point)

$\frac{1}{2}$ in/12 mm white pom-poms

Small disposable container

99-percent isopropyl alcohol

Ranger alcohol ink in Ginger

Copic marker in Cadmium Yellow (Y15)

9 millinery lily stamens

Pineapple heavy crepe

18-gauge cloth-covered stem wire

Lemon fine crepe

Chiffon extra-fine crepe

Design Master Tint IT spray paint in Pinkalicious (530)

Eye protection

Wire snips

Juniper extra-fine crepe

Awl

Templates (page 228)

1. **Preparing the ball**

   a. Insert the compass point into one end of the ball to draw a circle with a radius of 1¾ in/4.5 cm all the way around one end of the ball. With the floral foam knife, very carefully slice off the section inside the circle. Precision isn't that important—you just want the bottom of the ball to be flat.

   b. Use template A to cut eight segments from the foam sheet. Cut 3¼ in/8.5 cm lengths of the Fern/Moss doublette crepe parallel to the fold. Using the wedge sponge, spread a thin layer of tacky glue onto one side of a foam sheet segment. Place it in the middle of one of the doublette rectangles and press it down onto the paper.

   c. Cut the crepe around the segment, leaving a ¼ in/6 mm margin all the way around.

   d. Dot tacky glue over the margin, working 3 in/7.5 cm at a time. Fold the crepe over the foam sheet, adjusting it as you work for a smooth edge. Allow to dry.

   e. Repeat for the remaining segments.

2. **Building the cactus**

   a. Now you're going to glue the segments together to start building the cactus. The trick here is to avoid gaps in the segments while also not turning the outside into a gluey mess.

   b. Pin the point of one end of a segment to the top of the ball, opposite the middle of the base, and pin the other end to the bottom at the edge of the flattened base, using one pin on each side of the bottom of the segment. Cut off the lower end of the segment, even with the edge of the base. Squirt a line of glue up and down the strip, just underneath the edge of the first segment. Place the second segment right next to the first and on top of the joining segment, and pin it in place. Press down 2 in/5 cm at a time to help the glue set.

   c. Repeat to add the remaining segments. Don't worry if some segments are a little gapped or gluey. Whichever section is best can be the front of the cactus. Dot the whole cactus with chalk marker as shown.

   d. After an hour, remove all the pins.

1a.

2b.

1d.

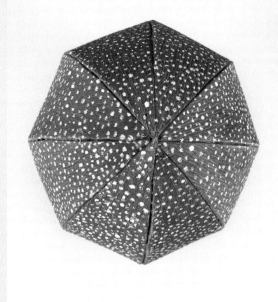

2d.

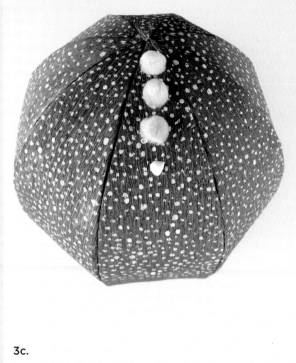

3c.

4a.

4d.

4e.

3. Adding the pom-poms

a. Now you're going to add a row of pom-poms down the middle of each segment. You can make a solid line or space them farther apart. The main thing is to try to space them evenly. However many pom-poms you decide to use per segment, multiply it by eight, so you'll have enough for the whole cactus.

b. Fill the small disposable container (a clean single-serving yogurt cup would be perfect) with 1 Tbsp isopropyl alcohol and 30 drops of the Ginger ink. Stir thoroughly. Submerge the pom-poms in the ink and let them fully saturate with dye. Allow to dry completely.

c. Carefully snip off about 40 percent of the pom-pom, creating a flat side to attach to the cactus. Glue on the pom-poms, holding each one in place for ten seconds so it adheres.

4. Making the flowers

a. Use the yellow marker to color three of the lily stamens. Bundle the stamens together with the tips even. Apply a tiny amount of glue ¾ in/2 cm from the tips of the lily stamens, and pinch them all together. Use a 2 in/5 cm stem strip from the Pineapple crepe to wrap the stamens to the tip of the wire stem (for wrapping instructions, see page 92), so the lily stamens stick out 1⅜ in/3.5 cm beyond the tip of the wire. Use template B to cut a fringe piece from the Pineapple crepe. Twist the fringes and then follow the instructions on page 92 for making confetti stamens with pollen from the Lemon fine crepe.

b. When the fringe is dry, dot it with glue below the glue line indicated on the template and, starting at the wider end, wrap it around the tip of the wire so the top of the fringe falls just below the bottom of the head of the lily stamen.

c. Cut an 18 by 20 in/46 by 51 cm rectangle of Chiffon crepe. Following the instructions on page 99, use the Pinkalicious spray paint to create lightweight horizontal stripes 5 in/12 cm apart on the rectangle. Cut across the top of each stripe to create strips to accordion fold for petals. Follow the instructions on page 87 to cut forty petals on the fold from the strips (using template C).

d. Apply glue to a petal below the glue line indicated on the template. Attach it to the center so the glue line on the petal lines up with the glue line on the

Pineapple fringes. Add another petal, slightly overlapping it with the previous one. Repeat until you've made it all the way around the first row. Apply a second row, staggering the petals so each petal in the second row shows in the space between two petals in row 1.

e. Using eye protection and wire snips, clip the stem to 3½ in/9 cm long. Finish the flower by following the instructions on page 92 to wrap the stem in Juniper crepe. (The back of the flower is intentionally chunky so it looks like a thick cactus stem.)

f. Use the awl to pierce a hole ½ in/12 mm from the center of the top of the cactus. Insert the flower stem into the hole and push it in to the point where the thick stem meets the cactus.

g. Repeat, adding two more flowers, distributed in a triangle pattern at the top of the cactus.

1b.

2b.

1a.

1d.

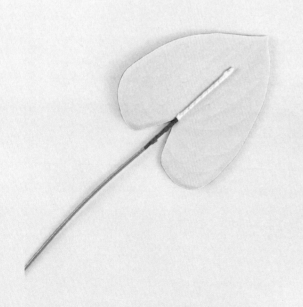

Anthurium

SEE PAGE 45

I had to really fight the impulse to make twenty different anthurium flowers to include here, because there are just so many neat spathe shapes and colors to play with. The templates I've included should get you started, but I think the best anthuriums are wonky and misshapen, so definitely try freehanding your own!

1. Making the spathe

a. Using template A, cut a spathe from the cardstock. (I've provided four additional spathe templates for variation, should you decide to make multiple flowers.) If the cardstock has any texture, make that the back side of the spathe. With the Mod Podge brush, apply a coat of the Mod Podge. Try to minimize streaks. Allow to dry completely.

b. Following the embossing directions on page 95, emboss the cardstock, using the pattern on template A1. Use the ¼ in/6 mm embossing tool for the edges and the heavier weight lines. Use the ¹⁄₁₆ in/2 mm (or similarly fine) embossing tool for the pattern between the lines.

c. Emboss and fold over a three-dimensional edge all around the spathe, following the instructions on page 96. Then, following the instructions on page 92, wrap the top 2 in/5 cm of the stem wire with the crepe that matches the cardstock. Wrap the next 1 in/2.5 cm below that with Juniper extra-fine crepe.

d. Dot the first 2 in/5 cm of the wrapped wire with glue and attach it down the middle of the back of the spathe so the point where the cardstock-colored crepe changes to green crepe is lined up with the bottom of the "V" that's formed where the two lobes of the spathe meet. Allow to dry.

2. Making the spadix

a. You'll construct the spadix by wrapping a wire with floral tape over and over to build up a thick spike. Choose floral tape that coordinates with the pastel color you're using. Pale colors work best with white tape, dark or jewel tones with black tape, and medium tones with beige, kraft-colored tape.

b. Wrap up and down the top 3 in/7.5 cm of the wire until it's about ¼ in/6 mm thick. Every few wraps, press the tip smooth. It will taper as you wrap, but if you'd like more pronounced tapering, begin at the bottom of the spadix, wrap the first 1 in/2.5 cm, and then wrap back down again. Repeat, wrapping ½ in/12 mm higher each time and then wrapping back down again. When you reach the top, wrap the whole spadix once or twice to smooth everything together. Wrap the 1 in/2.5 cm of wire below the bottom of the spadix with Juniper extra-fine crepe.

SUPPLIES

Scissors

Cardstock in pinks, greens, or very dark reds or purples

Mod Podge applicator brush

Mod Podge Gloss

Extra-thick foam sheet, ¼ in/6 mm thick

Embossing tools, ¼ in/6 mm and ¹⁄₁₆ in/2 mm

18-gauge cloth-covered stem wire

Crepe paper in any weight in a color similar to the cardstock

Juniper extra-fine crepe

Aleene's Original Tacky Glue

Floral tape in black, white, or beige

PanPastel in Permanent Red Tint (380.8), Violet (470.5), and Bright Yellow Green (680.5)

Soft brush

Eye protection

Wire snips

Templates (page 234)

c. Apply the pastel to the spadix with the soft brush. Rather than making brush strokes up and down the spadix, load the brush with color and then dab it on. For a bicolored spadix, like the white with green tip on my pale pink anthurium, dab the green heavier on the tip and lighter farther down to help blend with the white floral tape.

3. Building the flower

a. Carefully bend the stem of the spathe where it meets the cardstock to a 45-degree angle. Wrap the stem of the spathe and the stem of the spadix together with a stem strip of the Juniper extra-fine crepe, starting ¼ in/6 mm beneath the spathe and the spadix. You may want to wrap it twice if it doesn't seem quite secure. Trim the bottom with wire snips if they aren't even.

b. The finishing will depend on how you'd like to display the flower. I like the spadix to be at about a 30-degree angle to the spathe and the spathe to lie at a 140-degree angle to the stem.

2c.

3a., 3b.

Spider Orchid

SEE PAGE 46

This delicate orchid is beautiful by itself in a vase, and its arching habit makes it an especially nice addition to an arrangement. This project is a great chance to learn stem work, since all the blooms have to be added to a central stem without creating a lot of bulk.

1. **Prepping the petals**

   a. Use template B to cut five petals from the doublette. Completely color these petals using the Avocado marker. You may need to color both sides if the ink doesn't soak all the way through. Allow the ink to dry.

   b. Use template A to cut a labellum on the fold from the doublette (see page 87). With the Vanilla side facing up, speckle the labellum using the Aubergine marker, following the instructions on page 98. Speckle the petals next, dotting more densely at the base of the petal and more sparsely toward the tips.

   c. Gently scissor curl the petals into a "C" shape. Stretch either side of the "V" that makes up the bottom of the labellum. Scissor curl the bottom half of the labellum toward the White side, following the instructions on page 88.

2. **Building the flower**

   a. Cut a 2 by ¼ in/5 cm by 6 mm strip from the doublette. Dot the strip with glue and wrap the top 1 in/2.5 cm of wire two or three times, following the instructions on page 92 for wrapping stems. Color the top ½ in/12 mm of the wrapped wire tip using the White marker.

   b. Hold the labellum between your thumb and forefinger ½ in/12 mm from the point of the narrow end. With your other hand, pinch together the remaining ½ in/12 mm of the labellum. Dot glue on the pinched section and lay the wrapped wire tip on the glued labellum so the wire tip extends ¼ in/6 mm beyond the bottom of the pinched section. Press the pinched section around the wrapped stem to help the glue set. Add all five curled petals, following the instructions on page 91 for making a flower with five petals.

   c. Adjust the petals by pushing them away from the center. The labellum should protrude forward. Wrap the whole stem using the Juniper crepe, following the instructions on page 92.

   d. Repeat this process until you have a total of twelve flowers. (You can, of course, use more or fewer blooms.) The remaining eleven flowers should be built on 4 in/10 cm lengths of the stem wire.

SUPPLIES

Scissors

White/Vanilla doublette crepe

Prismacolor Premier marker in Avocado (PB-192)

Copic marker in Aubergine (V99)

Aleene's Original Tacky Glue

18-gauge cloth-covered stem wire

Copic marker in Wax White (G20)

Juniper extra-fine crepe

Floral tape

Eye protection

Wire snips

Templates (page 234)

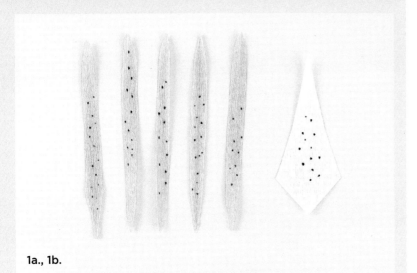

1a., 1b.

2c.

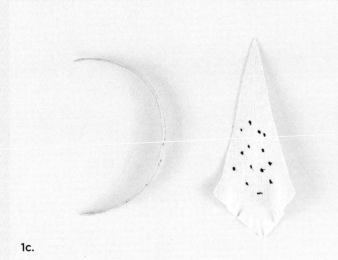

1c.

2b.

3c.

3d.

3d.

4a.

3. Building the branch

a. The 18 in/46 cm wire with the first flower is the main stem; as you build the branch, you'll place blooms on alternating sides of this stem. To prepare these flowers, bend them out to the side a little less than 90 degrees. The bend should be 2 in/5 cm behind the back of the flower. The flower on the 18 in/46 cm wire should face straight up and needs no bend. Six of the remaining flowers should face away from the stem and off to the left, and five should face away from the stem and off to the right.

b. By using 4 in/10 cm lengths of wire rather than just wrapping together a bundle of twelve 18 in/46 cm wires, you reduce bulk and keep the stem looking fairly slender and uniform.

c. Choose one of the flowers on a 4 in/10 cm stem that faces out to the right. Place it on the right side of the main stem, 2 in/5 cm back from what will be the central flower. (Make sure the flower you're adding is right-side up, with the labellum on the bottom, and that it faces away from the main stem.) Following the directions on page 92, wrap the two wires together.

d. Add a flower that faces left to the left side of the stem, 2 in/5 cm lower than the first right-facing flower but on the opposite side of the stem. (Again, make sure it's right-side up.) You'll notice that, even when wrapped to the main stem, the bottom of the 4 in/10 cm wire juts out a little bit. Choose another right-facing flower, and add it to the right side of the stem, positioning it so it falls a little bit higher than this bump and a little bit in front of it so it's somewhat disguised. Repeat, alternating sides.

e. When you've added all the flowers, you'll have a mess of wires of different lengths sticking out the bottom. Secure these by wrapping them tightly with floral tape. Use additional floral wires to lengthen this stem by slipping them up into the floral taped bundle and then wrapping down the stem to cover these added wires.

f. Using eye protection, snip the remaining wire. Wrap the stem in Juniper stem strips.

4. Finishing the flower

a. Bend the stem into an arch and adjust the flowers so they face out and slightly upward away from the branch. Smooth any petals that have been mussed during the building of the stem.

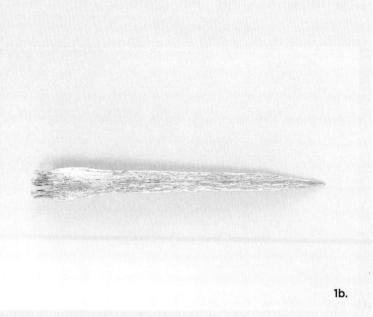

1b.

2c.

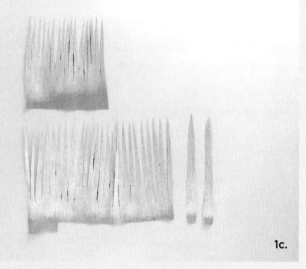

1c.

2d.

3b.

Blushing Bride Tillandsia

SEE PAGE 49

Paper air plants are great for adding interesting, delicate foliage to a paper flower arrangement. But they're also adorable displayed in the multiplicity of cool air plant vases, hanging cages, and planters that are available now that tillandsias have become so popular.

1. Preparing the leaves

a. Decide which side of the Olive Green doublette crepe you'd prefer for the front of the leaves (I've used the greener side). Cut pieces using the templates with this front side facing up. Using template A as a guide, cut a set of tillandsia leaves from the Olive Green doublette. Use template B to cut two individual leaves. With template C, cut a set of leaves from the Salmon crepe, choosing your preferred side for the front of the leaves (I've used the lighter side).

b. Use the wedge sponge to swipe the Green pastel onto both sides of the Olive Green and onto both sides of each individual B leaf. One side of the A leaf is longer than the other; starting on the shorter end, swipe the Pearlescent Red pastel over the top third of six of the leaves front and back. Starting on the longer side, swipe the Bronze pastel on the area under the indicator line on the bottom of the template (front and back), and then cut a fine fringe across the whole area under the line. Repeat for the bottoms of each of the individual leaves. Gently twist and untwist these fringes to make them look more root-like. At the bottom of each individual leaf, just above the glue line indicated on the template, stretch a little bowl in the leaf, using the directions for cupping on page 88.

c. To color the Salmon-colored set of leaves, swipe the Green pastel on the top one-third of all the leaves (front and back) and the Red pastel over the rest of the set of leaves.

2. Making the flowers

a. From the Lilac crepe, cut a rectangle for the stamens using template D. (You could also use a purple marker to color a piece of White heavy crepe.) Cut a 2 by 2 in/5 by 5 cm square from the Lemon crepe.

b. Fringe the D rectangle up to the glue line indicated on the template, aiming for between four and six stamens. If you've cut six across the strip and you have extra length, just snip it off.

c. Fold the Lemon square in half across the grain, then open it back up again. The fold line marks the depth of the fringe. Fringe across the square. Follow the instructions on page 92 for making confetti stamens. Dot glue on the D rectangle under the glue line indicated on the template, and roll the rectangle up. If it's easier, just twist the area up to the glue line.

SUPPLIES

Deep Olive/Olive Green doublette crepe

Scissors

Salmon/Dark Salmon doublette crepe

Cosmetic wedge sponge

PanPastel in Permanent Green Tint (640.8)

PanPastel in Pearlescent Red (953.5)

PanPastel in Bronze (930.5)

PanPastel in Permanent Red Tint (340.8)

Lilac heavy crepe

Lemon fine crepe

Aleene's Original Tacky Glue

Violet fine crepe

¼ in/6 mm dowel

Templates (pages 235–36)

d. From the Violet crepe, cut a rectangle on the fold for the outer petal using template E (see page 87). Following the instructions on page 88, scissor curl just the very top edge of the rectangle toward the back of the petal. Dot the right edge of the front of the petal with glue. Lining up the bottom of the stamens with the bottom of the petal, wrap the petal around the bundle of stamens. Dot the outer edge on the front of the petal with glue and press closed.

e. Repeat to make two additional flowers. Dot the bottom third of one of the flowers with glue and glue it to another flower so the tips line up. Glue the third flower to the first two, creating a little cluster.

3. **Building the tillandsia**

   a. The rest of the tillandsia is rolled up around these three flowers.

   b. Beginning on the pinker (rather than greener) end of the Salmon leaf set, wrap the strip of Salmon leaves around the bundle of flowers, making sure to keep the bottoms even. Repeat with the green leaf set, beginning with the pinker end. When you roll this set up, the roots at the bottom should form a circle.

   c. Add two leaves to make the bottom more realistic. Dot glue inside the area at the base of each leaf that you cupped. Attach the first leaf over the edge where the leaf strip ended. Make sure that the bottoms of the roots line up. Attach the second leaf opposite the first on the plant.

4. **Finishing the tillandsia**

   a. Use the ¼ in/6 mm dowel to curl back the leaves of the air plant. Start by curling the leaves on the outside of the plant and work your way toward the middle. The outer leaves should be curled back more dramatically and gradually become fairly straight at the center.

3b.

4a.

Lady's Slipper Orchid

SEE PAGE 50

Building the little purse on this orchid is one of the more challenging tasks in this book. It took some practice for me to get it right, and I would definitely suggest cutting two or three purse pieces to learn the basic instructions before you push yourself to complete a final draft version. (Also, though I didn't pick it for this reason, the darker crepe helps hide any little mistakes you might make, which is definitely a plus!)

1. **Building the pouch**

   a. Using the Sangria/Aubergine doublette crepe and following the instructions on page 87 for cutting out a half template on a fold, cut a template A piece. Dye it in the disposable container using the alcohol ink and following the instructions on page 97. (It's not a bad idea to dye two or three A pieces in case it takes a couple of tries.) Allow to dry.

   b. Stretch the bottom third of the purse, starting just above where the glue line is indicated on the template. Dot the area below the glue line with glue and twist the bottom of the purse. Allow to dry, then snip the twisted section just below the purse. Use your finger to press the twisted stub into the bottom of the purse, and to re-form any parts of the stretched purse bottom that may have collapsed.

   c. Use the skewer to curl the upper edges of the purse, following the instructions on page 88. To close up the purse, you'll glue the two side edges together. Dot a ⅜ in/9.5 mm strip of glue along the inner edge of one side of the purse. Line up the two edges of the purse so that they face each other, and press them together. Allow to try, then trim off most of the seam where you glued the purse shut, leaving enough of the seam in place to keep the purse from opening. Press the seam to one side on the back of the purse.

   d. Follow the instructions on page 92 for wrapping the stems with Cypress stem strips. Pinch the upper tip of the purse flat, dot the top ¼ in/6 mm with glue, and glue it onto the wire so ¼ in/6 mm of the wire extends past the place where the orchid is attached.

2. **Making the petals**

   a. Using template B, cut two side petals from the Sangria/Aubergine doublette. Use the soft brush to color the bottom, more curved, side of each petal (on the darker side) with the Magenta pastel. Use the purple marker to draw lines across this bottom section on each petal. Using the crystal drops, dot two rows of "warts" across the top of the petals. If you want to go really crazy with the details, cut little hairs for the leaf edges. Here are some potential sources of hair: the bristles of a cheap makeup brush, the black hair from a doll, or cheap false eyelashes.

1b.

1c.

1c.

1d.

2a.

4a.

5a.

6a.

b. If adding hairs, apply glue to the upper half of the upper edge of the petal and sprinkle the little hairs over the area. When the glue is dry, gently blow away any errant hairs. Add glue below the glue line indicated on template B, and add the petals on either side of the wire, just behind the purse. (Make sure they aren't upside down.)

3. Making the dorsal sepal

a. Using template C, cut a sepal from the Aubergine extra-fine crepe and brush Magenta pastel from the bottom, just short of the edges of the sepal. Draw lines with the Dark Bark marker as shown. Brush a very light coat of pastel over the top of the lines, just to help them blend in with the rest of the sepal. Dot glue on the petal below the glue line indicated on the template (on the front side of the petal) and glue it to the top of the stem, just behind the side petals. Press the sepal upward so it stands straight up above the rest of the orchid. Push the side petals out so they're on the same plane as the dorsal sepal. Push the pouch down so it's below the dorsal sepal.

4. Attaching the staminode

a. Cut a staminode from the Sangria/Aubergine doublette using template D. The darker side will be the front of the staminode piece. Very slightly scissor curl back the edges of the piece all the way, following the instructions on page 88. Make sure the template is right-side up. Dot glue in the middle of the back of the staminode and stick it on the tip of the wrapped wire.

5. Adding the bract

a. Use template E to cut a bract on the fold (see page 87) from the Cypress crepe. Cup the whole inside area (see page 88) and glue the piece around the wire, 2 in/5 cm behind the flower, so it points up toward the orchid. Using Cypress stem strips, wrap the stem a second time from the bottom of the bract to the bottom of the wire. Then cock the orchid forward so the bend is a ½ in/12 mm behind the flower head, and make sure the flower is facing front.

6. Making the leaves

a. Using templates F and G, cut one leaf on the fold (see page 87) from each using the green cardstock. Use the Mallow marker to add a mottled pattern to the leaves as shown in the photo. If this feels a little bit intimidating, you could also do a simple spotted pattern. Once the ink is dry, use the applicator brush to apply a coat of Mod Podge to each leaf. Allow to dry. Follow the instructions on page 96 to emboss the edges of one leaf and add points, placing the leaf on a foam sheet. Use the embossing tool to emboss a line down the center of the leaf. Bend the leaf around this centerline so it's folded vertically almost in half. Unfold. Wrap another one of the 18-gauge wires with Cypress stem strips. Dot glue on 4 in/10 cm of one end of the wire and stick it on the back of the leaf, using the embossed line as a guide. The place on the wire where the glue stops should be aligned with the bottom of the leaf. Repeat for the second leaf.

7. Assembling

a. Bundle and wrap the leaf wires and the orchid wire together (the bottom points of the leaves should meet the bottom of the flower stem). Wearing eye protection, clip the wires with the wire snips so you have 4 in/10 cm of the wrapped stem sticking out below the leaves.

b. Arrange the leaves and check to make sure the orchid is facing straight ahead and the main stem is sticking straight up. You can display the piece in a vase or insert the bottom ends of the wires into floral foam wedged into a pot, with freeze-dried moss around the top.

1a.

1c.

1b.

1d.

Spider Plant

SEE PAGE 53

Usually when you see a spider plant at the nursery, you're actually seeing multiple plants potted together. This is a more minimalist version, though you could absolutely make multiples of the project for a fuller plant.

1. Making the plantlets

a. Cut a total of eighteen leaves from the off-white cardstock using a combination of templates A through D. With the larger marker, draw a line along both edges of the leaf. With the finer marker, draw a fine line from the base of a leaf to the tip. This line should go to the right or left of the vertical centerline of the leaf. Flip the leaf, and repeat (the lines on either side of the leaf don't have to be identical). Repeat for all of the plantlet leaves.

b. Choose one of the smaller leaf pieces, and pinch the bottom ¼ in/6 mm of the leaf in half vertically. Dot the lower inside of the leaf with glue, and press it around the top ¼ in/6 mm of the 22-guage wire. Allow to dry. Wrap the leaf to the tip of the wire with floral tape, stretching as you wrap to activate the adhesive. Glue and wrap two additional leaves.

c. Now you'll add some root-like details to the bottom of the plantlet. Cut three to five very thin strips of the brown paper, ½ in/12 mm long. Twist them and then glue them evenly around the base of the plantlet, so that ¼ in/6 mm of the root extends beyond the bottom of the plant. Work in rounds to add the rest of the leaves, aiming to add three to five leaves each time around.

d. Now that you have your first plantlet, wrap the wire underneath, which will be the stem that attaches the plantlet to the mother plant. Following the instructions on page 92, wrap the 6 in/15 cm of wire below the plantlet with stem strips of the Buttercup crepe.

e. Once the plantlet is dry, use the dowel to curl the leaves, following the instructions on page 88 to curl the outer ones more dramatically and the inner ones less so. Bend the wire at a steep angle where it sticks out of the bottom of the plant. Repeat these steps to make another plantlet, this time using eye protection and wire snips to cut a 15 in/38 cm length of 22-gauge wire, wrapping 4 in/10 cm from behind the plantlet on this second stem.

f. Starting at the point where the Buttercup stem wrap ends on both wires, wrap the remaining lengths of the two wires together using single stem strips of the Buttercup crepe. The shorter stem should arch higher than the longer stem.

SUPPLIES

Scissors

Off-white lighter-weight cardstock

Faber-Castell PITT Big Brush Artist Pen in Earth Green (172)

Faber-Castell PITT Artist Pen in Earth Green (172)

Aleene's Original Tacky Glue

22-gauge cloth-covered stem wire

Kraft-colored floral tape

Lightweight dark brown paper of almost any kind

Buttercup heavy crepe

¼ by 12 in/6 mm by 30.5 cm dowel

Eye protection

Wire snips

18-gauge cloth-covered stem wire

Templates (page 238)

2a.

1f.

2a.

2. Making the mother plant

a. Repeat, except this time using templates E through G, building the plant around an 18-gauge stem wire, and omitting the tiny brown roots. When you have two-thirds of the leaves glued around the mother plant, use both glue and floral tape to wrap the bottom of the plantlet stem to the base of the mother plant. Add the remaining leaves, curl, and position the plantlet stem so it arches over the mother plant and then falls below it. The plantlets' stems should be bent into a gentle curve so they "float" up and away from the mother at the tips.

3. Finishing the plant

a. Trim the mother plant stem to your desired length, using wire snips and eye protection. You can snip it off altogether, leave just enough to anchor the plant in a pot filled with floral foam, or leave it long enough to stand in an opaque vase.

Long-Petaled Bulbophyllum

SEE PAGE 54

This plant was on my must-make list for a very long time. I wanted to make one both because it's such a beautiful and unusual plant and because it has so much potential as an element in a bouquet, either to drape down the edge of an arrangement or to arch over a bouquet.

SUPPLIES

Scissors

Pineapple heavy crepe

24-gauge cloth-covered stem wire

Aleene's Original Tacky Glue

Tsukineko Memento Dual Tip Marker in Sweet Plum (PM-506)

Tape

Vanilla extra-fine crepe

Prismacolor colored pencil in Process Red (PC994)

Cypress extra-fine crepe

18-gauge cloth-covered stem wire

Dark Green cardstock

Mod Podge applicator brush

Mod Podge Gloss

Foam sheet $\frac{1}{8}$ in/3 mm thick

Embossing tool, $\frac{1}{16}$ in/2 mm

Templates (pages 237)

1. **Making the flowers**

   a. Cut a 3 in/7.5 cm stem strip from the Pineapple crepe and, following the instructions on page 92 for wrapping stems, wrap the top ½ in/12 mm of the 24-gauge wire up and down three times. Cut one template A piece on the fold and two template B pieces from Pineapple crepe that has been fully stretched out. Following the instructions on page 88, scissor curl the A piece and glue it to the wire ¼ in/6 mm from the tip, using the glue line on the template as a guide. This piece marks the bottom of the center of the floret. Slightly curl both of the B pieces and glue them on either side of the center.

   b. Dot the tip of the wrapped wire and the side B pieces with the plum marker.

   c. Tape the top of template C2 to the bottom of template C1. Following the instructions on page 87 for cutting half templates on a fold, use this extra-long template to cut one flower piece from the Vanilla crepe. Next, use template D to cut one hood piece from the Vanilla crepe. Use the colored pencil to draw lines up and down the flower piece and hood, about ⅛ in/3 mm apart; these don't have to be perfectly straight or perfectly parallel. Repeat on the opposite side. Fold the flower piece, using the dotted lines on the template as a guide, so the edges meet in the middle, then overlap them, gluing the edge of one side so when you press it over the other side, the flower piece forms a tube. Twist both of the long, skinny tendrils at the bottom of the petal, twisting them lightly toward the top and more tightly near the bottom. Scissor curl the hood toward the center.

   d. Dot the hood with glue below the glue line indicated on the template, and attach it to the stem opposite the A piece. Dot the flower piece with glue below the glue line and attach it opposite the hood.

   e. Cut stem strips from the Cypress crepe, and wrap the flower stem for ¾ in/2 cm. Bend ¼ in/6 mm of the tip of the wire down by 45 degrees. Use template E to cut six bract pieces from the Cypress crepe. Lining up the piece so the glue line indicated on the template is just barely above where the wrapping ends, glue the bract to the stem. Repeat to make five more flowers.

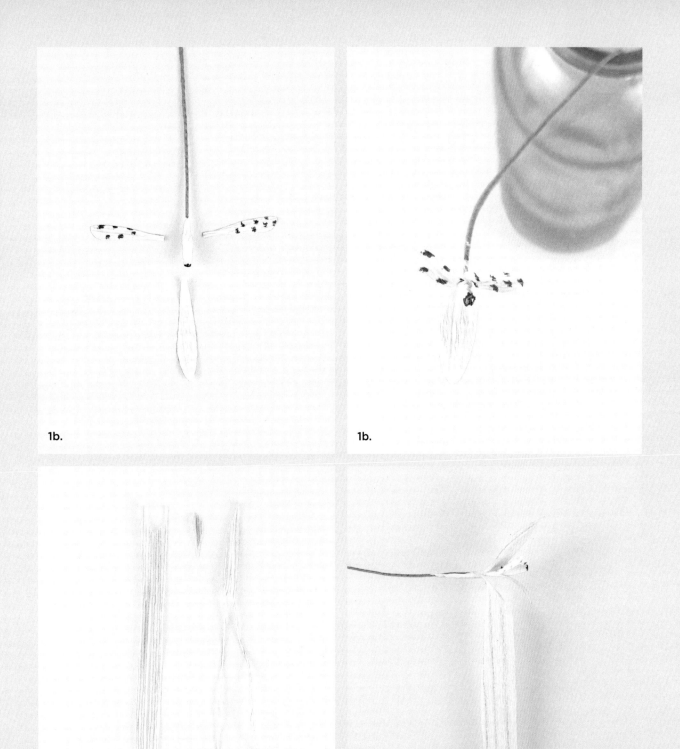

1b.

1b.

1c.

1d.

f. Gather the wires into a little bundle and wrap them together with Cypress stem strips to create the main stem. Spread out the flowers so they're all the same distance apart and all at the same height, forming a half circle that radiates out from the main stem. They should also tilt back, so the bottom half of the tubular part of the flower juts forward. Bend the main stem so it comes up behind the cluster of flowers and arches slightly before meeting the leaves the stems hang down from.

g. Repeat steps 1a. through 1f. to make a second stem of six flowers.

h. Wrap the individual stems together using 18-gauge stem wire to form the main stem of the sprig.

2. **Making the leaves**

a. Cut two template F leaves and two template G leaves from the Dark Green cardstock. Use the brush to apply a coat of the Mod Podge to each. Allow to dry. Follow the instructions on page 96 to emboss and point the leaf edges, using the foam sheet and embossing tool. Then emboss a line down the middle of the leaf. Bend the leaf around this line so it's folded almost in half vertically, then unfold. Wrap a full 18-gauge wire with Cypress stem strips. Dot glue on 4 in/10 cm of the wire, and stick it on the back of the leaf, using the embossed line down the center as a guide. The place on the wire where the glue stops should be aligned with the bottom of the leaf.

b. Gather all four of the leaf stems and the two flower stems and wrap them together with Cypress stem strips. You could treat this like a cut flower and just place the stem in a tall vase so the stem arches over the side and down below the plant, or you could use floral foam to anchor the stem in a hanging planter.

1f.

2b.

1a.

1b.

1c.

1c.

1c.

"Louise the Unfortunate" Rose

SEE PAGE 59

This rose, also known as 'Hume's Blush,' is one of those charming garden roses that are a little bit disorderly in the middle. If you find yourself with a perfect paper rose on your hands, you'll want to muss the middle with your fingers. If your rose turns out kind of kooky and eccentric, you will have done Louise proud!

1. **Making the flower**

   a. Use template A to cut a stamen fringe piece from the Nectarine crepe. Cut a fine fringe across the long end of this piece, cutting down to the glue line indicated on the template. Dot the fringe with glue below this line, and wrap it around the tip of the 22-gauge wire, so that the glue line meets the tip of the wire. Gently pat the stamens with your fingers so they become a little bit messy.

   b. Using template B, cut eleven petals on the fold (see page 87) from the Blush/Chiffon doublette. With the Blush side facing up, gently cup each petal, following the instructions on page 88. Fold the petal in half without creasing it, and twist the bottom using the glue line on the template as a guide for how far to twist. Glue these petals evenly around the stamens, making sure that the part of the petal where the two side edges meet faces the center. As indicated on the tempates, the glue line on the petal should meet the glue line on the fringe at the flower's center.

   c. Use template B to cut eighteen more petals from the Blush/Chiffon doublette. Cup each petal and, working in rounds of nine petals each, glue them evenly around the first row of petals, so that all the petals are at roughly the same height. Use template C to cut twenty-seven petals on the fold from the Blush/Chiffon doublette, which you'll use for the last three rows of petals. Cup the bottom two-thirds of each petal, and use your scissors to curl back the edges of each petal as shown, following the instructions on page 88. Add each row so that it falls slightly lower than the row in front of it.

   d. With template D, cut five calyx pieces from the Cypress crepe. Lightly scissor curl them. Dot them with glue under the glue line indicated on the template and add them to the stem where it meets the back of the flower. Following the instructions on page 92, use Cypress stem strips to wrap from behind the calyx pieces to the bottom of the wire.

2. **Making the buds**

   a. Cut a bud center petal from the Blush/Chiffon doublette using template E. Dot the bottom half of the Chiffon side of the petal with glue and position the 24-gauge wire at one edge, so the wire tip falls halfway up the petal. Wrap the petal loosely around the wire.

SUPPLIES

Scissors

Nectarine heavy crepe

22-gauge cloth-covered stem wire

Aleene's Original Tacky Glue

Blush/Chiffon doublette crepe

Cypress extra-fine crepe

24-gauge cloth-covered stem wire

⅝ in/16 mm wooden beads

PanPastel in Permanent Red Tint (340.8)

Small paintbrush or makeup brush

Templates (page 239)

Scrunch up the wrapped section. Dot the upper half of the scrunched section with glue and stick the wire through a wooden bead, pulling the scrunched section through so only 30 percent of the petal that is wrapped around the wire sticks through the top. Cut three template F petals. Place a petal on the bead so it's slightly higher than the rolled-up inner petal. Stretch the bottom two-thirds of the way around the bead, remove and dot the stretched area with glue, and put it back into place on the bead. Repeat with the remaining bud petals, overlapping them by about 30 percent.

b. Add five template D calyx pieces just as you did for the rose, and use stem strips to wrap from behind the calyx to the bottom of the wire. Make two more rose buds.

3. **Making the leaf sprigs**

   a. For each leaf sprig, wrap five 24-gauge wires with stem strips. Following the instructions on page 94 for making mitered leaves, build one template G leaf and four template H leaves.

   b. Place two H leaves on either side of a G leaf, about ½ in/12 mm below the bottom of the G leaf. Wrap the three stems together with stem strips for 1 in/2.5 cm. Wrap another set of template H leaves ½ in/12 mm below the first set. Continue to wrap the sprig stem with stem strips until you've covered the whole thing. Bend the leaves so the upper set forms a 45-degree angle to the main stem. The lower set should be more like 90 degrees. Repeat to make two more leaf sprigs.

4. **Assembling the stem**

   a. Wrap the rose, the buds, and two leaf sprigs together, 3 in/7.5 cm down the wire from the calyx of the flowers and buds and 1 in/2.5 cm below the lower set of leaves on the sprigs. Wrap to the bottom of the stem.

   b. Place the remaining sprig on the stem, 2 in/5 cm below the flower. Wrap to the bottom with stem strips.

5. **Finishing the stem**

   a. Arch the leaf sprigs a little bit so they look more natural, and bend the rose and bud stems to open up the branch a little bit. Using the pastel and the soft brush, add detail to one side of the stem and on the edges of some of the leaves.

1c.

3b.

4a.

SUPPLIES

Eye protection

Wire snips

22-gauge cloth-covered stem wire

Purple millinery stamens

Aleene's Original Tacky Glue

Scissors

Lilac extra-fine crepe

1¼ in/3 cm polystyrene ball

Eggplant heavy crepe

6 wooden skewers

Small awl

18-gauge cloth-covered stem wire

15 in/38 cm vinyl tubing, ⅜ in/1 cm
outer diameter

Juniper extra-fine crepe

Templates (page 239)

Allium

SEE PAGE 60

This one is really fun to see come together . . . until about three-fourths of the way through, at which point it becomes a big challenge to insert the last florets while holding the almost completed allium globe in your hand as you try not to rumple the petals. I have a trick to make this a little bit easier.

1. **Making the florets**

   a. Using eye protection and wire snips, cut the 22-gauge stem wire into ¾ in/2 cm lengths. Cut 2 millinery stamens in half. Dot the lower half of the stamens with a little bit of glue, then bundle them together. Dot a small amount of glue on the side of the wire and place it on the stamens so the tips extend ½ in/12 mm from the bottom of the wire. Cut a stem strip from the Lilac extra-fine crepe. Following the instructions on page 92 for wrapping wire, begin wrapping just above the point where the tip of the wire hits the stamens, then spiral down until the rest of the wire is covered.

   b. Use template A to cut five petals from the Lilac extra-fine crepe. Twist the bottom ⅛ in/3 mm of each petal and follow the instructions on page 91 for attaching five-petal flowers.

   c. It's difficult to say how many florets you'll need, as minor variations in spacing can have a big effect on the total. I recommend making ten or twenty at time, adding those to the foam ball, and then repeating until the ball is covered.

2. **Making the allium center**

   a. Use template B to cut a rectangle from the Eggplant heavy crepe. Follow the instructions on page 89 for stretching crepe around a shape (with no extra paper on the bottom). Poke one skewer into the bottom of the ball and one on the top. Insert a third skewer into the side of the ball, midway between the top and bottom. Insert a fourth skewer opposite the third. Insert a fifth skewer halfway between the third and fourth horizontally and halfway between the first and second vertically. The sixth skewer should be opposite the fifth. Having these six skewers placed like this will make it a little bit easier to hold the ball in place while you poke the wire into it. Be sure to have five florets ready to replace the skewers when you remove them (the sixth will be replaced by the stem).

3. **Adding florets**

   a. Start applying florets around the bottom of the ball, leaving a ½ in/12 mm gap between the bottom skewer and the florets. To insert them into the ball, carefully pierce the ball with the awl, and then insert the floret into the hole. There's no need to get the spacing exactly right, but I aim for all the florets to be about

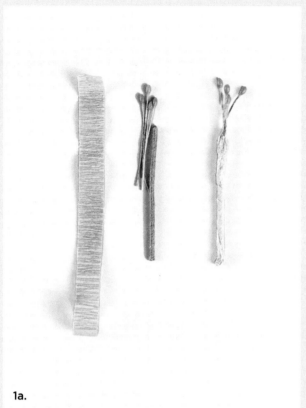

1a.

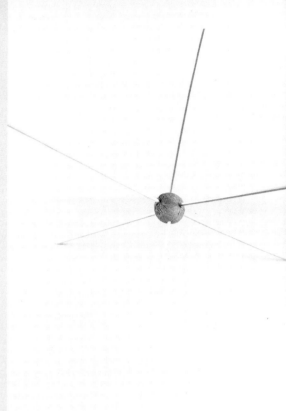

2a.

1b.

3a.

⅛ in/3 mm from each other. The important thing is to have a fairly even distribution of florets around the ball. As the ball gets more and more covered, I find it easier to hold the floret by the stamens as I push it into the ball. When the whole ball is covered, remove the six skewers one by one, replacing five with a floret; remove the bottom skewer last. Cover the top 1 in/2.5 cm of two 18-gauge stem wires with glue and insert them into the bottom of the ball.

b. Wrap the top 3 in/7.5 cm of the vinyl tubing in Juniper crepe stem strips. Push the tubing up over the wire and up against the ball. If the stem won't stay rigid, insert another stem wire into the tubing, and even a third if necessary. Wrap the rest of the tube with stem strips. At the bottom of the stem, fold the stem wire back over onto the wrapped tubing, which will help hold the tubing in place.

4. **Finishing the allium**

a. Take a few minutes to adjust any wires that are leaning at odd angles, any petals that have become crumpled, or stamens that have become bent.

b. After having put in so much work on this project, be very careful to keep it out of bright light to minimize fading.

3b.

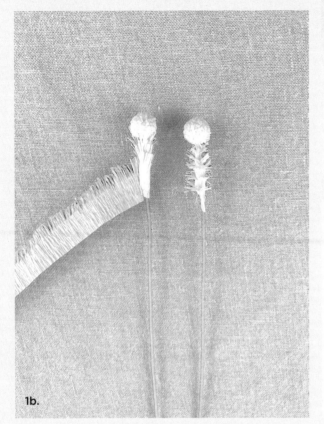

1b.

2b.

2b.

2c.

Black Hollyhock

SEE PAGE 63

I've designed a 3 ft/90 cm hollyhock to make it more practical for displaying at home, but feel free to size it up. I once built one on a thrifted fishing pole so the stem could be taken apart to make transporting it easier. But it turns out there's a piece of hardware called a dowel connector that allows you to make tall, portable hollyhocks. Having been so proud of my innovative use of fishing tackle, I was a bit sheepish at the discovery, but I quickly rallied when I realized I would never again have to strip a reel off a decrepit fishing pole.

1. Making the flower center

a. Use the yellow marker to color the spun cotton ball pale yellow. Cut a 2 in/5 cm square of the Pineapple crepe, stretch it all the way out, fold it in half, and fringe across the rectangle up to the fold. Cross-cut the fringes to make confetti, following the instructions on page 92. Use the wedge sponge to smear glue all over the ball and then roll the ball in the confetti. Let dry.

b. Use template A to cut a fringe piece for the hollyhock center from the Pineapple crepe. Stretch the piece all the way out, and fold according to the line indicated on the template. Fringe to the fold line. Fold the strip so the fringe is at a 90-degree angle to the rest of the rectangle. Wearing eye protection and using wire snips, cut two wires to 9 in/23 cm and one wire to 18 in/46 cm. Dot glue below the fringe line, and, starting ¼ in/6 mm below the tip, wrap it 1 in/2.5 cm down one of the wires just as you would a stem strip. (See instructions for wrapping wire on page 92.) Repeat with the remaining two wires.

c. Use your finger or a wire to help push any stamens that are lying against the wire away from the stem. Following the instructions on page 92, dip the fringes in glue and then in the confetti. Dot the tip of the wire with glue and insert it into the cotton ball.

2. Making the flowers

a. Cut five template B petals from the Black crepe, using the instructions on page 87 for cutting petals on a fold.

b. Follow the instructions on page 90 to crinkle the petals. Open up the petal, stretching out some of the crinkles but leaving about half in place. Use a dowel to curl the bottom third of the petal toward you, following the instructions on page 88. Then use it to curl the upper two thirds of the petal away from you. Dot glue on a petal, using the template glue line as a guide, and attach it at the base of the flower center. Add the additional four petals, overlapping them by 20 percent. Once all your petals are curled, gently stretch them along their upper edges for additional frills.

SUPPLIES

Copic marker in Barium Yellow (Y00)

¼ in/6 mm spun cotton ball

Scissors

Pineapple heavy crepe

Cosmetic wedge sponge

Aleene's Original Tacky Glue

Eye protection

Wire snips

22-gauge cloth-covered stem wire

Black fine crepe

¼ by 12 in/6 mm by 30.5 cm dowel for curling

Four 1 in/2.5 cm foam balls

Four 1¼ in/3 cm foam balls

Forest Green extra heavy crepe

¼ by 36 in/6 mm by 90 cm dowel for stem

Templates (page 239)

c. Go around the flower, dowel-curling the top third of the petals and curling the areas where the petals overlap as though you were curling a single petal. Use template C to cut five calyx pieces on the fold from Black crepe. Dot glue on each piece, using the glue line on the template as a guide, and apply them around the flower evenly. Bend the stem so the flower will be at a right angle to the main stem when attached. Repeat to make two more flowers.

3. Making the buds

a. Following the directions on page 89 for stretching crepe around a shape, cover four 1 in/2.5 cm foam balls and one 1¼ in/3 cm foam ball with the Forest Green crepe. Repeat with Black crepe on the remaining three 1¼ in/3 cm balls. Use calyx template C to cut five green calyx pieces for each of the smaller balls, and template D to cut five green calyx pieces for each of the larger balls. Cup all the calyx pieces, following the instructions on page 88. For each bud, pierce the ball with stem wire at the midpoint between the ends that you glued in place. Dot glue on the calyx pieces using the glue line on the template as a guide and distribute them evenly around the ball, making sure to strategically position them to hide the gathered section of crepe on either side of the ball. Wrap the bottom of the bud and 15 in/38 cm down the wire with stem strips. Bend the stem so the bud will be at a right angle to the main stem when attached.

4. Making the leaves

a. You'll need a total of three template E leaves, three F template leaves, and four template G leaves from the Forest Green crepe. Cut the three E leaves. (Don't stretch the paper out before making the leaf.) For the F and G leaves, follow the instructions on page 94 to make mitered leaves. The small and medium leaves should be built on 9 in/23 cm lengths of wire. Two of the large leaves should be made on an 18 in/46 cm wire. Wrap a 3 in/7.5 cm length of the stem wire with a stem strip from the same crepe, and glue it to the back of each leaf, under the seam, making sure the tip of the wire doesn't stick out beyond the leaf. Bend the stem so the leaf will be at a right angle to the main stem when attached.

5. Assembling

a. To make the most of the flowers, buds, and foliage, you'll put them all on the front or sides, leaving a bare "back" of the stem. (If you need a hollyhock that can be seen from all angles, you can certainly apply them all the way around the stem.) Cut a stem strip from the Forest green Crepe, and wrap the top 2 in/5 cm of the dowel. Bundle the dowel and three of the smaller buds together, so the middle bud is just a little bit higher. Wrap them all together with a stem strip. Beginning 1 in/2.5 cm below this, add a small leaf toward the front on the left side of the stem. Add a small bud 1½ in/4 cm below this point on the right side of the stem. Add another small leaf 1 in/2.5 cm further down, on the left toward the front. Then, 1 in/2.5 cm below this point, add the large bud with the green center to the front with the last small leaf 1 in/2.5 cm below it. Another 1 in/2.5 cm below this point, add a flower on the right toward the front. Another 1 in/2.5 cm below that, add a medium leaf toward the front on the left. Another 1 in/2.5 cm below that, add a large bud on the left front. Finally, 2 in/5 cm below that, add a medium leaf on the right.

b. Add a large bud 1 in/2.5 cm below the flower on the front. Add the last medium leaf 1 in/2.5 cm below on the left. Add a large leaf 1½ in/4 cm farther down, on the right. Place a flower 1 in/2.5 cm below that on the left side, toward the center. Next, place a large leaf 1½ in/4 cm below that on the left. Then add a large bud 1½ in/4 cm down the stem on the left. Add a large leaf 1½ in/4 cm farther down on the left. Another 1 in/2.5 cm below that, add the next flower on the right side toward the center, and 1½ in/4 cm below the flower, add a large leaf on the left.

3a.

4a.

5a.

Itoh Peony

SEE PAGE 64

I've used spray paint to try to capture the watercolor quality of this peony's petals. I find that coloring a few different sheets of the extra-fine crepe with different amounts of color helps create subtle, organic shading. For multiple flowers, it would be beautiful to mix more heavily colored peonies with more faded ones.

SUPPLIES

18-gauge cloth-covered stem wire

Aleene's Original Tacky Glue

⅝ in/16 mm spun cotton flower bud

Scissors

Pineapple heavy crepe

Pale Yellow-Green heavy crepe

Golden Yellow heavy crepe

Chiffon extra-fine crepe

Design Master Tint IT spray paint in Pinkalicious (530)

Copic marker in Dark Bark (E49) or similar dark brown marker

Juniper extra-fine crepe

Eye protection

Wire snips

Templates (page 240)

1. **Making the center**

   a. Dip the end of the stem wire into the glue and insert it into the hole in the bottom of the spun cotton flower bud. This will be the peony's seedpod. Let dry.

   b. Use template A to cut a frill piece from the Pineapple crepe. Stretch out each rounded section across the top to give it some body. Stretch the piece around the seedpod, following the instructions on page 89. Scrunch the A piece around the top of the seedpod to secure the frills into place.

   c. Cut a 1¼ by 1½ in/3 by 4 cm rectangle from the Yellow-Green crepe and dot it with glue. Stretch it around the seedpod so the upper edge of the rectangle reaches to the point where the little frills radiate from the seedpod. Snip off any excess.

2. **Making the stamens**

   a. Use template B to cut a stamen section from the Golden Yellow crepe. Cut fairly chunky fringe up to the glue line as indicated on the template. Twist the fringes.

   b. Dot the fringe with glue right up to the glue line. Starting at the wider end, wrap this fringe piece around the wire stem, making sure that the glue line hits right up under the seedpod.

3. **Preparing the petals**

   a. Spray the Chiffon crepe with the spray paint in rows spaced at least 5 in/12 cm apart. (See tips for working with spray paint on page 99.) For row 1, cut one C template, two D template, and two E template petals. For row 2, cut three F template and two G template petals.

   b. With the marker, draw an upside-down teardrop in the middle of the bottom half of the petals from templates C through E, as shown on the templates. Add these markings to only those petals, not to the second row petals, since they won't be visible behind the first row.

   c. Gently stretch each petal around the upper edge and cup it all over so the whole petal forms a shallow bowl. (See instructions for cupping and stretching on pages 88 and 89.)

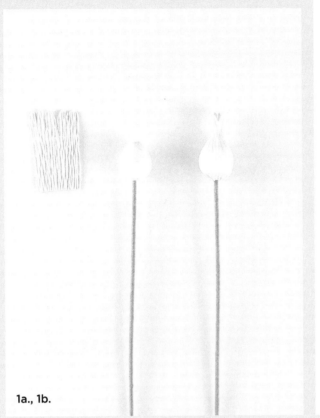

1a., 1b.

2a., 2b.

1c.

3b.

4b.

5a.

4. Adding the first round

a. The one trick to this round of the Itoh peony is placing the petals so the markings on each one are visible. Once you've attached the first petal, each additional petal should be placed to the right just far enough over that you can still see the marking on the petal you're attaching.

b. Following the instructions for adding five petals on page 91, attach one C petal, one D petal, one E petal, one D petal, and one E petal. The petals should overlap just a little bit.

5. Adding the second round

a. Place the first F petal just to the right of the last row 1 petal. Then add one G petal, followed by another F petal, followed by a G petal, and finally an F petal. Add petals evenly around the flower, overlapping them by 10 to 20 percent. For fuller flowers, cut more petals and repeat the second round as many times as you like.

6. Finishing the flower

a. Cut three template H pieces and three template I pieces on the fold from the Juniper crepe (see page 87). Gently cup the H calyx pieces, dot the bases with glue, and distribute them evenly around the stem. Curl the tips of the I pieces a little bit, and glue them in the spaces between the H pieces. Wrap the stem with Juniper stem strips, following the instructions on page 92.

b. To make a sprig with two flowers, make a second peony and wrap the bottom half of the two flowers together with a Juniper stem strip so they meet 4 in/10 cm below the back of one of the flowers and 3½ in/9 cm below the back of the other flower.

c. Using template J, cut two foliage pieces from the Juniper crepe. Apply a small amount of glue to the bottom ½ in/12 mm of the foliage piece and apply it to one stem, smoothing the glued section onto the stem, about 2 in/5 cm from the back of the flower. (Feel free to adjust.) Apply the second foliage piece to the other flower, 3½ in/9 cm from the back of the flower.

d. Using eye protection and wire snips, snip the bottom of the sprig to your desired length.

1b.

1c., 1d.

3a.

1f.

Opium Poppy

SEE PAGE 67

Made from a wooden bead wrapped in green crepe, with pale green chenille sewn in stripes all the way around, the seed head is the star in this flower. Pair it with red, pink, white, or purple petals.

1. Creating the center

a. Cut a 1½ in/3.8 cm by 1¾ in/4.5 cm rectangle from the Ivory crepe. Following the instructions on page 99, spray the crepe with the Basil spray paint to color the whole thing. Allow to dry. Follow the instructions on page 89 to stretch the rectangle around the bead, making sure to keep the holes in the bead at the top and bottom of the strip. Glue in place.

b. Color a 10 in/25.5 cm length of the chenille pale green using the Copic marker. Once the glue has dried on the crepe-covered ball, thread the chenille through the tapestry needle. Starting at one end of the bead (this will be the bottom), insert the needle into the bead and draw it up through the top of the bead. Insert the needle again through the bottom and draw it again up through the top. You've now created a vertical chenille stripe on the outside of the bead. Repeat all the way around the bead, keeping the tension fairly tight. I usually shoot for around nine stripes, but you can do from as few as six to as many as twelve. Once you've finished sewing the stripes, draw the needle once more up through the bottom and up through the top. Pull the chenille fairly tight and clip it right at the surface of the top of the bead.

c. Cut two stem strips across the grain of the painted square. Following the instructions on page 92 for wrapping stem wire, wrap the upper 3 in/7.5 cm of the stem wire with stem strips made from the painted crepe. Cover the top ½ in/12 mm of the wire with a thin coat of glue and gently insert it into the bottom of the bead. The chenille on the inside of the bead will adhere to the paper around the stem and hold things in place.

d. Use template A to cut a stamen piece from the Aubergine extra-fine crepe and template B to cut a pollen piece from the unpainted Ivory crepe. Follow the instructions on page 92 to make confetti stamens. (In this case, you'll add the pollen to the stamens before attaching them to the wire.)

e. Dot glue on the bottom of the stamens below the glue line indicated on the template. Position the strip so this glue line butts up against the bottom of the bead. The stamens will be either level with the bead or a little higher.

f. Wrap the stamen strip around the bead, keeping a little tension in the strip. It will be a little loose around the stem wire, so once

SUPPLIES

Scissors

Ivory extra-heavy crepe

Design Master Colortool spray paint in Basil (676)

1 in/2.5 cm wooden bead

Aleene's Original Tacky Glue

White miniature chenille (I buy mine from my local fly fishing shop)

Copic marker in Wax White (G20)

Tapestry needle

18-gauge cloth-covered stem wire

Aubergine extra-fine crepe

¼ in/6 mm dowel

Black fine crepe

PanPastel in Magenta (430.5)

Cosmetic wedge sponge

Templates (page 241)

you've wrapped the whole strip, scrunch the bottom around the wire and up into the bottom of the bead.

g. Use your fingers or the dowel to curl the stamens toward the center. (See page 88.)

2. **Preparing the petals**

   a. Following the instructions on page 87 for using half templates, cut two C petals and two D petals from the Black crepe. Following the instructions on page 99, swipe the Magenta pastel with the wedge sponge in the direction of the grain to cover both sides of the petals. (It actually looks better if the color is a little bit streaky.)

3. **Assembling the flower**

   a. Follow the instructions on page 89 to create a gentle ruffle across the tops of the petals, and the instructions on page 90 to crinkle the petals. Open up the petals almost all the way, uncrinkling them until there's only a little pleating left. Follow the instructions on page 88 to create a gentle, allover cup. Follow the instructions on page 91 for attaching four petals. Apply the C petals first, dotting glue under the glue line and wrapping the base of the petal two-thirds around the bead. Repeat for the D petals.

   b. Once the glue has dried on the petals, follow the instructions on page 92 for wrapping the stem in green-painted crepe.

4. **Finishing the flower**

   a. Take a moment to adjust the petals—depending on your desired finished flower, you might want to stretch the petals horizontally a bit so they'll cup toward the center, or use the dowel to make the curling a bit more dramatic.

5. **Color variations**

   a. The other two color variations I've made use Cyclamen and Orchid fine crepe. I've added markings using a Copic marker in Dark Bark (E49), drawing upside-down trapezoids that start at the base of the petal and reach two-thirds of the way up the petal.

3a.

3a.

Red Hot Poker

SEE PAGE 68

This red hot poker flower is built from the top down. The florets grow larger and more yellow as you move down the stem, and the flowers on the bottom show their stamens. Each template builds a floret in its own state of bloom.

1. **Cutting the petals**

   a. The color specified (for example, the Red-Orange from the Orange/Red-Orange doublette) is the color that should go on the outside of the floret. Keep careful track of which petals go with which templates.

   b. Cut twelve template A petals from the Red-Orange crepe. Cut twenty-two template B petals from the Red-Orange crepe. Cut fourteen template C petals from the Red-Orange crepe. Cut fourteen template D petals from the orange crepe. Cut twelve template D petals from the Gold crepe. Cut twenty-eight template E petals from the Yellow crepe. (Glue is applied to the reverse side of each petal.)

2. **Making the florets**

   a. Place an A piece on the table, Red-Orange-side down. Dot glue across the diagonal edge of the piece and also across the opposing short side.

   b. Roll up this floret, beginning on the shorter side. To make this easier, begin by folding the shorter side of the piece over onto the light orange side by about ⅛ in/3 mm. Continue to roll, stopping just before you reach the opposite, longer side. Dot this edge with glue, and press the little roll closed.

   c. While the glue is still wet, gently pinch the floret flat and pinch all around the tip to create a little point, then blunt the end by patting it with your fingers.

   d. To shape the back half of the floret and to get it ready to attach, twist what was the lower triangle section of the piece up to the line shown on the template.

   e. Templates B through D have an area for fringe that sticks up beyond the main part of the template and runs only partway across the top of the template. That allows the fringe to curve over the end of the bulkier section. Glue across the fringe and round it gently with your fingers.

   f. Template D has a notch taken out of its diagonal edge. This "dart" reduces bulk at the joint where you'll pinch the floret, allowing it to bend over farther. Pinch six of these florets into more acute angles as they are attached lower on the stem. The remaining six florets will point downward at an even steeper angle, so we'll reinforce each

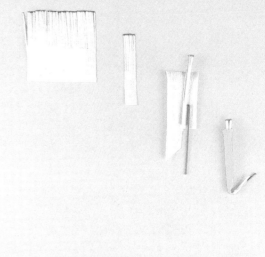

2i.

2b.

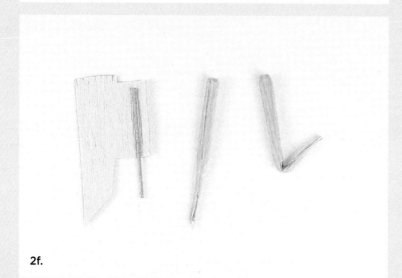

2f.

3a., 3b.

3b.

floret with wire. Using eye protection and wire snips, snip six lengths of 22-gauge wire, each 1½ in/4 cm long. Dot the shorter side of a template D piece with glue, and place the wire on top of the glue, so that the bottom of the wire is even with the bottom of the long-end of the piece. Repeat for the five remaining florets.

g. Template E is for florets that have already bloomed. Because these are lowest on the stem, they should point downward more than the others and reinforced with wire.

h. Cut a 1¾ by 6 in/4.5 by 15 cm rectangle from the Cream/Yellow crepe. Follow the instructions on page 98 to color one of the long edges of the rectangle with the Cadmium Yellow marker. Finely fringe the rectangle along this edge, cutting the fringe about 1 in/2.5 cm deep.

i. Snip this rectangle into sections about six stamens wide. Each section is a set of stamens for a template E floret. (If you run out of stamens, just make another fringed rectangle.) Twist the bottom half of this stamen set, dot it with glue, and glue it onto the short side of the E piece, so the bottom of the stamen set is even with the bottom of the short side. Using eye protection and wire snips, snip twenty-eight lengths of 22-gauge wire, each 1½ in/3.8 cm long. Place one of these wires on the short side beside the stamen set. The tip of the wire should reach halfway up the short side. Roll up the floret. Push back the fringes around the upper edge of the petal.

j. Repeat until you've built all the florets from the petals you've cut.

3. **Assembling the flower**

a. Cut a ¼ by 6 in/6 mm by 15 cm strip across the grain of the Orange/Red-Orange doublette. Dot the lighter side (the Orange side) with glue. Following the instructions on page 92 for wrapping stems, wrap the tip of the 18-gauge stem wire three times with the Orange strip.

b. Dot the twisted section of an A floret with glue. Line up the tip of the wire with the tip of the floret, and press the glued section onto the stem. Repeat with two more A florets, distributing the three florets evenly around the tip of the wire. From here, you'll spiral down the wire, adding the florets in the order specified in 1b. It's difficult to apply them with

perfect regularity, so I aim to place about six as a round, and I try to put each new floret slightly to the left of one in the preceding row.

c. Gently position and reposition these as you go to achieve some balance. Once you've used up all the florets, arrange so the florets are bent closest to the stem at the bottom and closest to the tip at the top.

4. **Finishing the flower**

a. If you find any bare patches you'd like to fill in, you can build an appropriately sized floret for that section of the stem, snip off the twisted section, and glue the floret directly into the empty space.

b. For the stem, cut a 15 in/38 cm length of the tubing. Slip it over the stem wire and wrap the top 3 in/7.5 cm with Juniper stem strips using the instructions on page 92. Slide it all the way up to the base of the flower. Wrap the remaining tubing with Juniper stem strips. (If the wire isn't holding the tubing straight, insert another 18- or 22-gauge wire into the tubing.) Bend the wire sticking out of the bottom of the tube over so it lies flush against the tubing, pointing up toward the flower. This will keep the tubing in place. If you wish, you can wrap the wire against the tubing with stem strips.

c. To add a little bit of color variation to the florets, use the soft brush to apply the Orange pastel to just the tips of the dark Orange florets.

1a.

1b., 1c.

1c.

1d.

Deadly Nightshade

SEE PAGE 73

Although these delicate nightshade sprigs would add lovely texture mixed with larger blooms in an arrangement, I love them best all by themselves. I chose a simple stem for this project, but you could also connect multiples together for a delicate wreath or make a bundle of stems and hang them upside down as if to dry.

1. **Making the flowers**

   a. Cut two of the white millinery stamens in half, then trim them to ¾ in/2 cm lengths. Dot the lower half of the stamens with a small amount of glue and then bundle them together. Dot glue on the side of the stem wire and place it so the tips of the stamens extend ½ in/12 mm beyond the tip of the wire. Secure the stamens to the wire by wrapping with a 3 in/7.5 cm strip of Dark Green crepe.

   b. Cut a 3 by 9 in/7.5 by 23 cm rectangle from the Fern crepe. (The long side of the rectangle should go across the grain.) Following the instructions on page 99 for working with PanPastel, use the wedge sponge to swipe short strokes of the pastel across the top of the rectangle. Lift the sponge at the bottom of the stroke to create a soft edge.

   c. Position template A on the stripe so the color runs from the tip of the petal to about the middle of it. Cut out five A petals on the fold (see page 87). Cup the bottom half of the petal above the glue line indicated on the template, following the instructions on page 88. Scissor curl the top edge of the petal, following the instructions on page 88. Repeat this to make four more petals. Dot each petal below the glue line indicated on the template and attach them around the stamens, overlapping the petals by 50 percent.

   d. With template B, cut five calyx pieces on the fold from the Cypress extra-fine crepe. Curl them back slightly at the tip, then attach them to the wire, behind the petals. Cut a stem strip from the Cypress crepe. Following the instructions on page 92 for wrapping wire, wrap 1 in/2.5 cm from behind the calyx. Repeat to make the second flower.

2. **Making the berries**

   a. Add glue from the tip of a wire to about ⅛ in/3 mm down. Insert the wire into the hole in a cotton ball. Allow to dry. Color the entire ball with the Dark Bark marker. When dry, apply two or three coats of the Mod Podge using the brush. When the ball is completely dry, add five calyx pieces in the same way you did for the flower (see step 1d). Wrap the wire behind the calyx for 1 in/2.5 cm using Cypress stem strips. Repeat to make the second berry.

SUPPLIES

Scissors

Small white millinery stamens

Aleene's Original Tacky Glue

22-gauge cloth-covered stem wire

Dark Green fine crepe

Fern extra-fine crepe

Cosmetic wedge sponge

PanPastel in Magenta Extra Dark (430.1)

Cypress extra-fine crepe

¼ in/6 mm spun cotton balls

Copic marker in Dark Bark (E49)

Mod Podge Gloss

Mod Podge applicator brush

Eye protection

Wire snips

Templates (page 242)

3. Making the leaves

a. Follow the instructions on page 94 for making mitered leaves from the Cypress crepe. You will need two of template B, one of template C, one of template D, two of template E, two of template F, two of template G, two of template H, two of template I, one of template J, and two of template K. The leaves should be built on 4 in/10 cm stems, except for one of the template B leaves, which should be built on an 18 in/46 cm wire.

4. Building the stem

a. First, attach two template E mini leaves to the base of one template B and one template C leaf. Dot glue below the glue line of the mini leaf and glue it onto the front of the B and C leaves, so the glue line falls at the very base of the leaf. Bundle a B leaf with a C and D leaf on either side. Wrap the wires together for 1 in/2.5 cm using the Cypress crepe. Using eye protection and wire snips, snip the wire from the C and D leaves. Wrap until the snipped ends are covered. The wire from leaf B will run down the entire stem, forming a backbone for the nightshade.

b. For this next cluster and the clusters farther down the stem, you'll need a larger leaf, a smaller leaf, two mini leaves, and a flower or berry. In general, if berries and flowers will be on the same stem, the flowers should be higher on the stem and the berries lower. In each cluster, the larger leaf will be placed highest, the smaller leaf will be placed lowest, and the flower or berry will be in the middle.

c. In the second cluster, you'll use one template F leaf for the large leaf, one template B leaf for the small leaf, two template G leaves for the mini leaves, and a flower or berry. Both the larger and smaller leaves will have a mini leaf glued on just as you did for the tip of the stem. The base points of the leaves should meet the wire, as should the point on the berry or flower where the wrapping stops.

d. Bundle the leaves and flower around the stem (slightly higher than the snipped ends from the previous cluster) and wrap them all together for 1½ in/4 cm. Using eye protection and wire snips, snip all but the B leaf wire.

e. Repeat for the third cluster, this time using one template H (large leaf), one template F (small leaf), and two template I (mini leaves). Wrap this cluster for 2 in/5 cm.

f. Repeat for the fourth cluster, this time using one template J for a large leaf, one template H for a small leaf, and two template K mini leaves. Wrap this cluster for 2½ in/6 cm. For any additional clusters you'd like to add, use the same templates and spacing, basically making additional fourth clusters.

g. Arrange the leaves, posing the clusters so they angle toward opposite sides of the stem, with the large leaf on top, the flower or berry in the middle, and the small leaf on the bottom. All the leaves should face forward.

2a.

4a.

4d.

4f.

Cobra Lily

SEE PAGE 74

My pale sarracenia with spotted throat is only one of the cobra lily's many variations in color and pattern. I encourage you to adapt this pattern to other sarracenia varieties and experiment using some of the color techniques on pages 96–99.

1. Cutting

a. Cut one template A piece from the doublette crepe, using the fold technique on page 87. (The area below the cobra lily "head," which is the widest part of the template, I'll call the shoulders.)

2. Coloring

a. In the disposable container, make a solution of ¼ cup/60 ml isopropyl alcohol and ¼ teaspoon alcohol ink. Stir until the ink is evenly mixed. Dip the A piece bottom first into the dye solution so the area from the bottom of the lily to ¾ in/2 cm below the shoulders is dyed. Lay the lily on a protected surface to dry. (The dye will wick up the lily as it dries, adding color to the cobra lily neck and the bottom of the head.)

b. After the lily is dry, choose the side with the color you like best. (I usually choose the side where the ink is darker.) Place this side face up and use the Copic Blender Marker to smooth the line between the ink and the uncolored paper. Flip the lily over. Following the speckling directions on page 98, use the plum marker to speckle from about ½ in/12 mm from the very top of the lily to ½ in/12 mm below the shoulders.

3. Assembling

a. Following the dotted line on the template, fold each side toward the middle of the lily. Dot the edge of the underside of the folded area on the left with glue. Working 1 in/2.5 cm or so at a time, gently press the folded area on the left over the folded area on the right, adjusting to make the fold even as you go.

4. Shaping

a. Following the instructions on page 89 for stretching crepe, gently stretch the area between the pointed tip of the lily and the widest point on either side of the head. Following the directions on page 88 for curling, use a skewer to curl the rounded areas on either side of the lily head toward the back of the lily, creating wings. Gently uncurl them a bit so they aren't curled too tight. Pinch the top of the lily, creating a little valley fold, and scrape the throat (or the point on the inside of the lily where the lily head meets the shoulders) a few times to pitch the head forward. Adjust until you like the overall form.

SUPPLIES

Scissors

White doublette crepe

A disposable container, long and wide enough to fit the cobra lily template

99-percent isopropyl alcohol

Adirondack alcohol ink in Lettuce

Copic Colorless Blender Marker

Tsukineko Memento Dual Tip Marker in Sweet Plum

Aleene's Original Tacky Glue

Skewer

Templates (page 242)

OPTIONAL BASE

4½ in/11 cm foam half ball

Variety of small amounts of brown and gray paper in any weight, crepe or otherwise

Spray bottle with water

Toothpicks

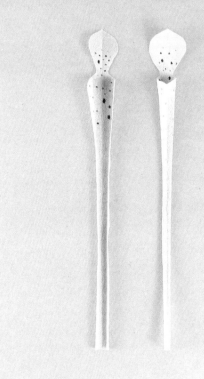

3a.

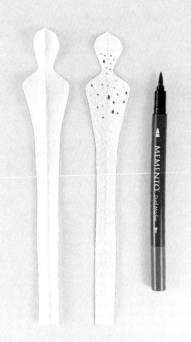

2b.

4a.

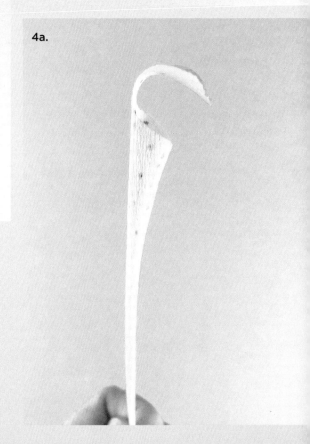

5. **Styling tip**

   a. Repeat to make multiple lilies. To display your cobra lily colony, cover the half ball with "dead leaves" made with brown and gray paper. First, add texture to the paper by misting it lightly with water and crumpling and smoothing it a few times to create finer crinkles. Press the paper flat and fold it in half. Cut a variety of simple half-leaf shapes. Open up the folded leaves and, for authenticity, cut little insect bites in the leaves if you like.

   b. Glue the dead leaves onto the rounded area of the half ball. Stab a cluster of toothpicks around the center of the half ball, and slip the bottoms of the lilies over the toothpicks. Position the lilies so they all face front.

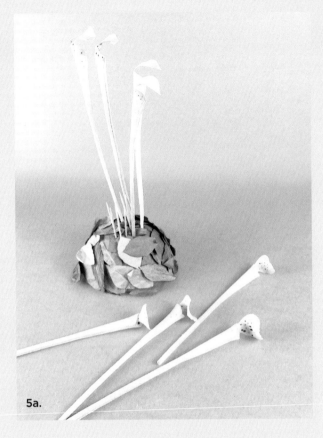

5a.

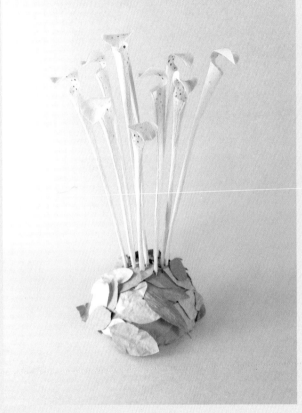

1a.

1a.

1c.

1d.

King Protea

SEE PAGE 78

The soft, fuzzy center eluded me for months. I tried felt, flocking, novelty spiderwebs, feathers, yarn, fleece, silk—nothing worked. When I finally figured out that wool roving could be added in a way that felt true to a king protea, I was elated.

1. **Making the center**

   a. Cut a template A shape from the cereal box. Dot tacky glue on the side of the wedge with a glue line, and glue it on top of the opposite edge, making sure to align the glue line and the opposite edge, creating a cone. When the glue is dry, paint the cone with the white paint. Allow to dry. Use masking tape to tape the cone to the half ball. Slip the 15 in/38 cm tubing over the stem wire and push it right up into the bottom of the half ball. If you prefer a straighter stem, insert one or two additional wires into the tubing. Bend the wire back over the tubing at the bottom of the stem to secure the tubing. Wrap the tubing in Juniper stem strips (see page 92).

   b. Cut a 9 by 13 in/23 by 33 cm length of Pineapple crepe (the longer side runs across the grain), so that the top of the rectangle has a ridge running across it. The row across the top, underlined by the ridge in the paper, is where you'll attach the wool roving to form the fuzzy section.

   c. Approximately 4 in/10 cm from the top of the rectangle is another ridge line. Fold the rectangle along this ridge line. Stretch along the whole length of the fold (see page 89). Open up the rectangle, and use the wedge sponge to apply tacky glue all over the top half of the rectangle on the inside. Then stretch the rectangle around the flower center, lining up the stretched fold with the edge of the half ball. Dot tacky glue on one edge of the rectangle and overlap the sides slightly to glue the rectangle closed.

   d. Gather the crepe paper around the cardboard cone, and gently press it onto the cone to help it adhere. Try to keep the little pleats in the paper an even size all the way around the cone. Allow the glue to dry. Paint the "fuzzy section" with the white paint. Allow to dry.

   e. Working 2 to 3 in/5 to 7.5 cm at a time, smear tacky glue on the top 2 in/5 cm of the cone with the wedge sponge. Place the roving over the glue so it runs in the same direction as the grain of the crepe. Make sure the lengths of roving are longer than the glued area they lie across. Press the roving into the glue. Repeat all the way around the cone and allow to dry completely. Trim the wool roving by holding your scissors parallel to the cone and snipping one area at a time, leaving some of the excess length at the tip of the cone. Gather up all the excess length and twist it. Snip the

SUPPLIES

Scissors

Cereal box

Aleene's Original Tacky Glue

White acrylic paint

Masking tape

Polystyrene half ball

15 in/38 cm length of vinyl tubing, ½ in/1.5 cm outer diameter

18-gauge cloth-covered stem wire

Juniper extra-fine crepe

Pineapple heavy crepe

Cosmetic wedge sponge

Wool roving (white)

White doublette crepe

Design Master Colortool spray paint in Burgundy (710)

Design Master Tint IT spray paint in Pinkalicious (530)

Design Master Colortool spray paint in Perfect Pink (780)

Foam paintbrush

FolkArt Home Decor Chalk Paint in White Adirondack (34150)

Skewer

Templates (pages 242–43)

1e.

2c.

1e.

2d.

twisted section where it meets the tip of the cone and pat it smooth with your fingers. Gather the excess paper below the rounded base of the flower around the stem and wrap with Juniper stem strips (see page 92 for wrapping stems).

2. Making the petals

a. Cut an 18 in/45 cm length of White doublette. Cut it in half lengthwise. Following the instructions for spray painting crepe on page 99, spray each of the halves across the top with the Burgundy spray paint. Then spray a stripe of Pinkalicious beneath the Burgundy stripe, overlapping the two stripes by 50 percent, and spraying all the way across the paper. Repeat, adding a stripe of Perfect Pink beneath the Pinkalicious.

b. Cut the petals on the fold (see page 87) from these lengths of paper, positioning the templates on the sprayed stripes so all of the petals get some of each of the three colors. You will need twenty-eight template B petals for rows 1 and 2, twenty C petals for rows 3 and 4, and twenty template template D petals for rows 5 and 6. Using the foam paintbrush, paint the reverse side of each of the petals with a thin coat of White Adirondack paint. When the petals are dry, use the skewer to curl the edges of the petals inward, following the instructions on page 88.

c. Dot glue on a B petal below the glue line indicated on the template. Align the petal so the glue line falls just below the edge of the half ball, and glue the petal to the side of the half ball. Repeat with thirteen more B petals, spacing them about ¼ in/6 mm apart all around the center. For row 2, place more B petals ¾ inch/18 mm lower than the petals in row 1. Stagger the petals so that the row 2 petals are placed between the petals in the first row.

d. Next is the third row of petals, leaning out, away from the ball. Dot one template C petal with glue below the glue line indicated on the template. Attach it to the center so that the tips of the petals fall about 1 in/2.5 cm below the tips of the petals of the last row. When attaching the third row of petals, don't worry about lining them up with the row of petals in front; just glue them fairly evenly around the center. (I find it helpful to think of it as five petals on each side of the center.) Repeat, adding nine more template C petals. Using the rest of your C petals, add a fourth round about 1½ in/3.5 cm below row 3. Using ten of your template D petals, add row 5, about 1 in/2.5 cm below row 4. Repeat to

make row 6, attaching the last ten of your D petals. Place these petals so that about 1 in/2.5 cm falls below the center onto the tubing. Wrap the petal bottoms to the tubing, using Juniper stem strips. Continue wrapping until the whole stem is covered.

Snake's Head Fritillary

SEE PAGE 81

To achieve the fritillary's signature checkerboard pattern, I used a white paint pen to draw parallel columns of irregular, slightly oblong dots. Since the white paint doesn't fully cover the dark paper, some of the of the paler mauve shows through, creating a more subtle color pattern. I find that dots that look deliberate persuade the eye. So speckle with conviction!

SUPPLIES

Scissors

Limon extra-heavy crepe

Lily millinery stamens

Copic marker in Wax White (G20)

Small yellow millinery stamens

Aleene's Original Tacky Glue

22-gauge cloth-covered stem wire

Dark Red or Magenta doublette crepe paper

Disposable gloves (optional)

Ranger alcohol ink in Currant or similar

Small disposable dish

Newspaper or paper bag

Hampton Art Chalk Marker (fine point)

Moss extra-heavy crepe

Eye protection

Wire snips

Templates (page 242)

1. Building the center

a. Use template A to cut a rectangle from the Limon crepe. Stretch the rectangle all the way out horizontally, pulling open all the crinkles. This rectangle will give you enough fringe for several flowers.

b. Crease and then unfold the bottom of the rectangle along the glue line shown on the template. Cut a fine fringe across the top of this rectangle, cutting each fringe up to the glue line (see page 92 for more tips on cutting fringe).

c. Snip a ⅜ in/1 cm section of the fringed rectangle (you'll snip all the way from the top of the fringes to the bottom of the rectangle). Gently twist and untwist the fringes and then press them straight with your fingers.

d. Color two lily stamens using the white marker. Bend one small yellow stamen in half. On the section of fringed rectangle you snipped off, dot glue below the glue line shown on the template. Lay two lily stamens down the middle of the fringe piece. The tips of the stamens should extend all the way beyond the tips of the fringes.

e. Place two yellow stamens on top of the fringed lily stamens, so the yellow stamen tips fall a bit lower than the lily stamen tips. Glue the stamens together below the glue line shown on the template. Trim any stamen strings sticking out below the bottom of the fringed rectangle to create a clean edge. Dot glue across the bottom of the stamens and fringe. Lay the stem wire on top of the fringe and stamen stack. The tip of the wire should fall just slightly above the glue line.

f. Wrap the rest of the fringe piece around the wire. It's fine if this involves some gathering and smooshing. Just press the wrapped stem all around to smooth it out.

1c.–1f.

3b.

2a., 2b.

2. Making the petals

a. Using template B, cut six petals from the Dark Red or Magenta crepe for each flower you'd like to make. Work in a well-ventilated area and wear gloves, unless you don't mind red fingers. Squirt the Currant alcohol ink into the disposable dish and dip the petals in the ink. When the petals are completely saturated, place them on newspaper or a paper grocery bag and allow them to dry completely.

b. Following the directions on the chalk marker, practice a little bit on a scrap of crepe paper until you feel comfortable with the flow of the pen and the size of the dots. Apply columns of similarly sized dots right down the center of the petal, from the tip to the base. Add additional columns on either side of this first column until you've covered the entire petal. Try to make the columns fairly close together and fairly regular, but don't stress about it. Let the petal dry.

3. Shaping the petals

a. Working from the bottom of the petal up to the little corner at the tip, gently stretch the petal horizontally. (For stretching tips, see page 89.)

b. Note the markings on template B: there's a tiny shaded area on the top right of the petal and two dotted lines, one on the upper right of the petal and one on the upper left. Dot a very small amount of glue on the petal based on the shaded area of the template. Tuck the glued section under the upper left area of the petal, lining up the edge indicated by the template with a dotted line on the upper right side of the template. The point on the left side will extend slightly beyond the point on the right side. Wipe off any excess glue.

4. Attaching the petals

a. The petals are applied in two rounds of three. Dot the pointy tip of the petal with a small amount of glue. Position the petal so the tips of the stamens fall about two-thirds of the way up the petal. Press the glued section of the petal onto the wire. Add the remaining five petals, following the instructions on page 91 for applying two rows of three petals. To finish the flower, use the Moss crepe and follow the instructions on page 92 for wrapping the stem. Bend the stem wire into an arch, so the flower faces downward.

b. To make a leaf, cut a ⅛ by 4 in/4 mm by 10 cm strip of Moss crepe parallel to the grain. Taper one end of this strip and round the tip. Curl the leaf a bit on the tapered end (see page 88 for curling instructions). Dot a very small amount of glue on the bottom of the leaf and attach it to the stem, 1½ to 2 in/4 to 5 cm from the flower. Repeat, adding a second leaf opposite the first.

c. To create a sprig with two flowers, make a second flower. With the two flowers facing in opposite directions, use a stem strip of the Moss crepe to wrap the bottom third of the two stems together.

d. Wear safety glasses as you use the wire snips to trim the bottom of the stem to the desired length.

4a.

4a.

1a.

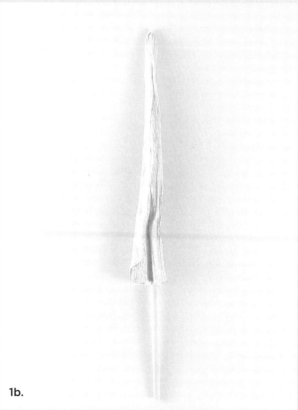

1b.

2a.

2b.

Corpse Flower

SEE PAGE 82

It was so hard to decide on a size for this project. Although an 8 ft/2.4 m corpse flower would be thrilling, I felt a smaller one would be more accessible to crafters not willing to give the flower its own bedroom. I finally settled on this 10 in/25 cm version, which is as strange and charming as the full-size plant, but still fits on a mantel. (If you decide to go for it and make a full-size corpse flower, you have my blessing, as long as you send me a photo!)

1. **Making the spadix**

    a. Using template A, cut one spadix piece on the fold (see page 87) from the cardstock and one from the Pear crepe. Cut off a ½ in/12 mm strip across the bottom of the cardstock piece. Roll the cardstock piece into a funnel with the point on top. Spray it with the spray adhesive, and cover it in the pear crepe, stretching slightly for a tight fit. The Pear crepe will be higher on top than the cardstock. Snip a short, vertical fringe along the top of the Pear crepe, and smear tacky glue inside the fringed area of the funnel. Pinch the fringes into a point, pinching all around to make it even as the glue dries. Blunt the tip of the spadix by tapping it with your finger.

    b. When the spadix is completely dry, squeeze and crumple it so it has the same crooked appearance as a live corpse flower. When the spadix is fully distressed, poke the dowel up into the inside of the funnel and restore a basic funnel shape.

2. **Preparing the spathe**

    a. Following the instructions on page 87 for cutting a half template on a fold, cut one template B spathe from the Bordeaux crepe and one from the Ivy crepe, positioning the template so the top of it falls on the white area of the ombre, and the bottom falls on the bottom green edge. Spray the more intensely colored side of the Ivy paper with the spray adhesive. Place the Bordeaux piece on top of the Ivy and push down on the two layers, spreading your hands around the paper to help set the glue.

    b. Once the spathe is dry, follow the instructions on page 89 to ruffle the entire upper edge of the spathe. Cut 1½ in/3.5 cm deep slits across the upper edge at 1 in/2.5 cm intervals. Following the instructions on page 88, scissor curl the top 2 in/5 cm of the spathe toward the green side. Cup the bottom 2 in/5 cm of the spathe all the way across, using the directions on page 88. Dot glue on the curved lower edge of one side of the spathe, and glue it to the other curved edge overlapping the other side by about 1 in/2.5 cm all the way down to the base of the plant.

SUPPLIES

Scissors

White cardstock

Pear extra-fine crepe

Elmer's Multi-Purpose Spray Adhesive

Aleene's Original Tacky Glue

¼ in/6 mm dowel

Bordeaux heavy crepe

Ivy Ombre heavy crepe

Green floral tape

Floral foam

Flower pot

Freeze-dried moss

Templates (page 244)

2c.

3a.

c. Insert the dowel into the spathe, so that 2 in/5 cm sticks out the bottom. Use floral tape to wrap the bottom 1 in/2.5 cm of the spathe to the dowel, and keep wrapping to cover the remaining length of the dowel.

3. Finishing

a. To "plant" the corpse flower, wedge the floral foam into the flower pot and stick the dowel into the foam. Place the spadix funnel on top of the dowel. Add freeze-dried moss around the top of the pot.

ACKNOWLEDGMENTS

I AM DEEPLY GRATEFUL TO THE FOLLOWING PEOPLE:

My editor, Rachel Hiles, for her patience, grace, wisdom, and tireless encouragement. My agent, Cindy Uh, who made all of this happen. I truly would not be here without your guidance, insight, passion, and tenacity. Kira Corbin and Alice Gao, for making my plants and flowers look so stylish and magical. Lizzie Vaughan, for creating such a gorgeous vision for this book. Elizabeth Lockhart, for her keen eye and generous styling advice. Chelan Kelly, for her expert flower-making assistance and general good company. My flower buddies, Lynn Dolan, Quynh Nguyen, Jennifer Tran, and Tiffanie Turner, for inspiration, commiseration, advice, and paper-flower humor. Karima Cammell, for planting and nurturing the seeds of this paper flower renaissance. Anne Zazzi, Grace Kim, Jan Halvarson, Brittany Jepson—women I admire so much, who encouraged and supported me early on. Grace Bonney, for being something like a fairy godmother to me and for years of beautiful, thoughtful, inspiring work at Design*Sponge. Jim Adams, Doug Mao, and Harry Shaw, whom I had hoped to thank in another project, for all their kindness. The women at Impress Cards and Crafts, who have supported me since I nervously taught my first flower class and cheered me on all this way. Jane Liaw-Grey for seeing me through every step of this project. My kids, Ben and Evie, for a thousand silly moments that kept me going (meow). Finally, my husband, Andrew, who somehow MacGyvered our family through the past year with ingenuity, generosity, and panache. Nobody sacrificed more than you did to make this happen, and nobody could have been a better sport about it.

GLOSSARY

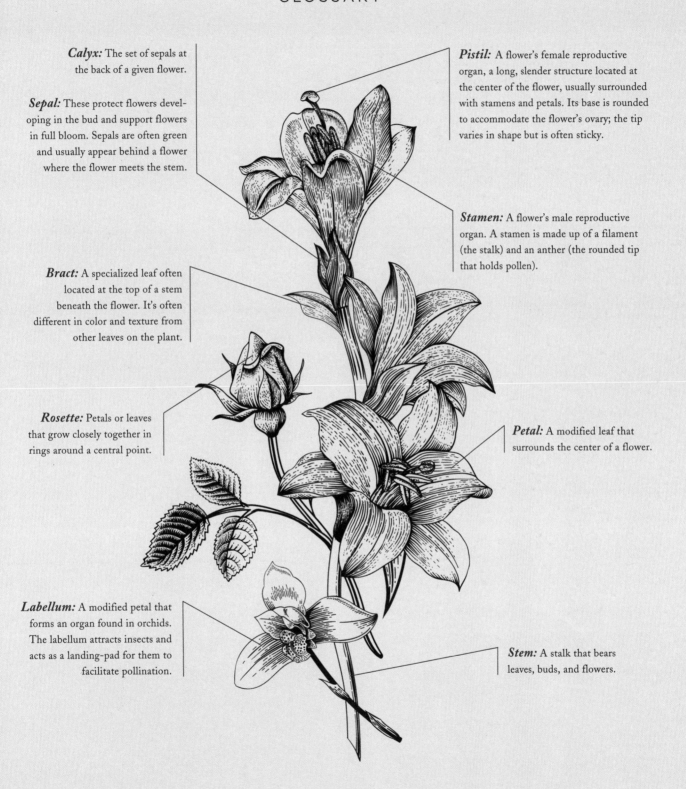

Calyx: The set of sepals at the back of a given flower.

Sepal: These protect flowers developing in the bud and support flowers in full bloom. Sepals are often green and usually appear behind a flower where the flower meets the stem.

Bract: A specialized leaf often located at the top of a stem beneath the flower. It's often different in color and texture from other leaves on the plant.

Rosette: Petals or leaves that grow closely together in rings around a central point.

Labellum: A modified petal that forms an organ found in orchids. The labellum attracts insects and acts as a landing-pad for them to facilitate pollination.

Pistil: A flower's female reproductive organ, a long, slender structure located at the center of the flower, usually surrounded with stamens and petals. Its base is rounded to accommodate the flower's ovary; the tip varies in shape but is often sticky.

Stamen: A flower's male reproductive organ. A stamen is made up of a filament (the stalk) and an anther (the rounded tip that holds pollen).

Petal: A modified leaf that surrounds the center of a flower.

Stem: A stalk that bears leaves, buds, and flowers.

Templates

HOW TO USE

To use these templates, you can photocopy these pages or use tracing paper to trace the template. Then cut the template shapes from the photocopy or tracing paper—these shapes will be your template pieces. I recommend labeling these pieces so you can remember what's what. To use these template pieces to make your crepe pieces, you can either trace the shape of the cut-out template pieces with a pencil onto the crepe and then cut the crepe, or you can simply hold the template piece against your crepe and cut around it.

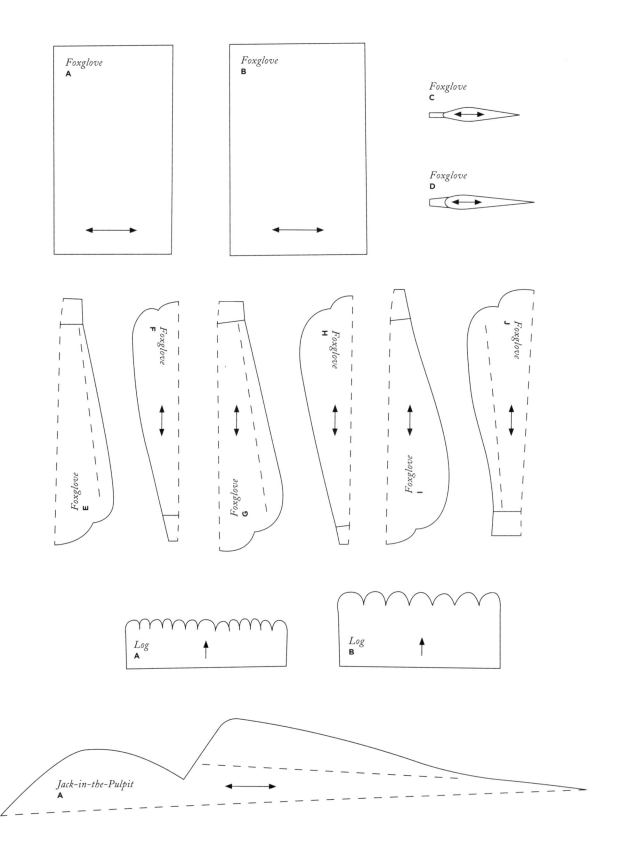

Foxglove
A

Foxglove
B

Foxglove
C

Foxglove
D

Foxglove
E

Foxglove
F

Foxglove
G

Foxglove
H

Foxglove
I

Foxglove
J

Log
A

Log
B

Jack-in-the-Pulpit
A

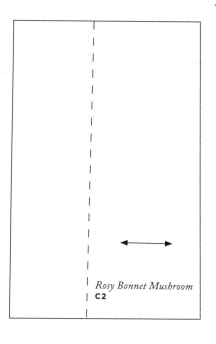

Rosy Bonnet Mushroom
C2

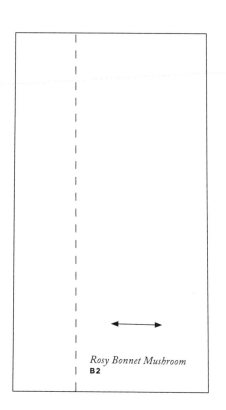

Rosy Bonnet Mushroom
B2

Rosy Bonnet Mushroom
C1

Rosy Bonnet Mushroom
D1

Rosy Bonnet Mushroom
B1

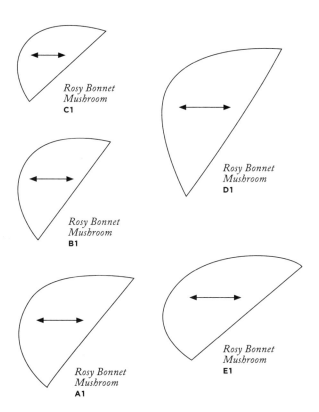

Rosy Bonnet Mushroom
A1

Rosy Bonnet Mushroom
E1

Rosy Bonnet Mushroom
A2

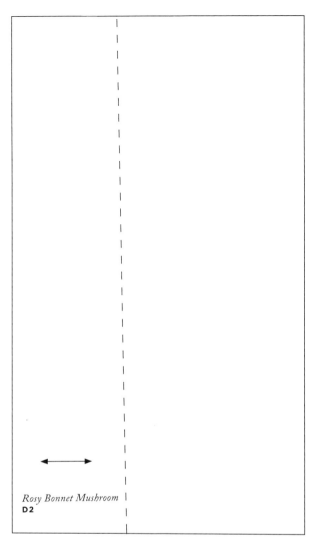

Rosy Bonnet Mushroom
D2

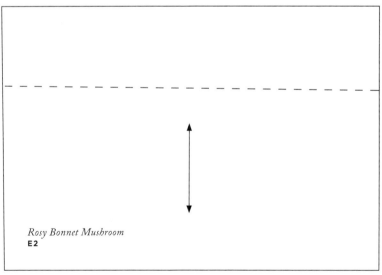

Rosy Bonnet Mushroom
E2

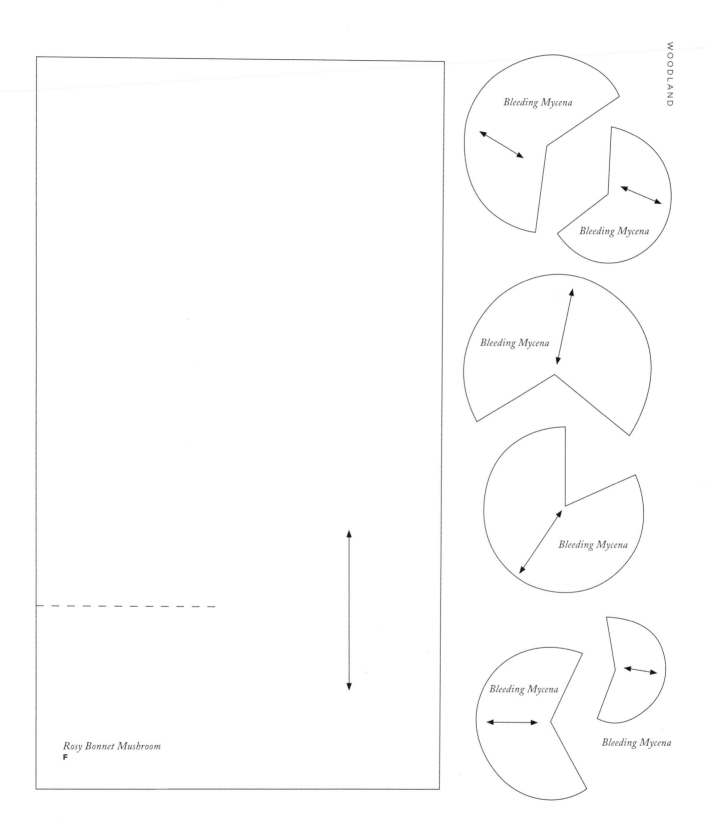

Bleeding Mycena

Bleeding Mycena

Bleeding Mycena

Bleeding Mycena

Bleeding Mycena

Bleeding Mycena

Rosy Bonnet Mushroom
F

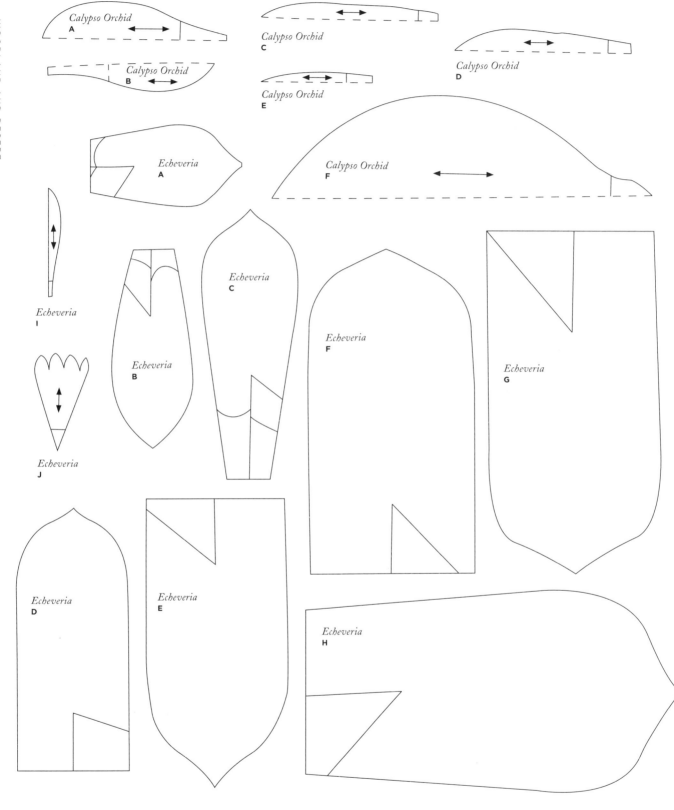

Calypso Orchid
A

Calypso Orchid
C

Calypso Orchid
D

Calypso Orchid
B

Calypso Orchid
E

Calypso Orchid
F

Echeveria
A

Echeveria
I

Echeveria
B

Echeveria
C

Echeveria
F

Echeveria
G

Echeveria
J

Echeveria
D

Echeveria
E

Echeveria
H

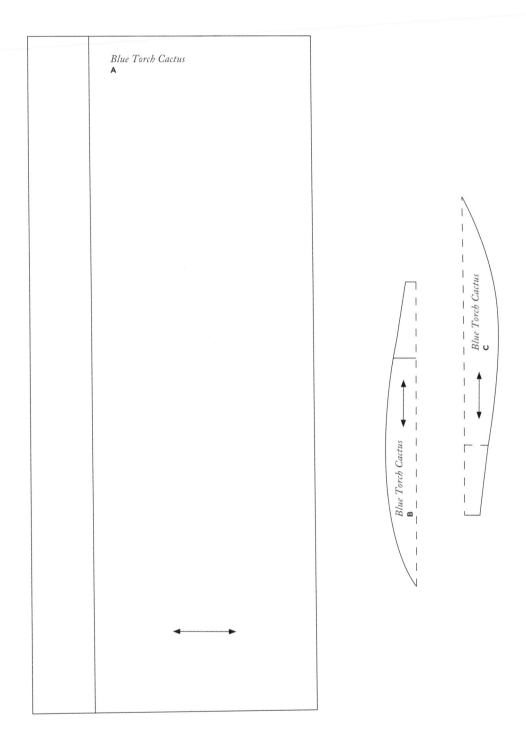

Blue Torch Cactus
A

Blue Torch Cactus
C

Blue Torch Cactus
B

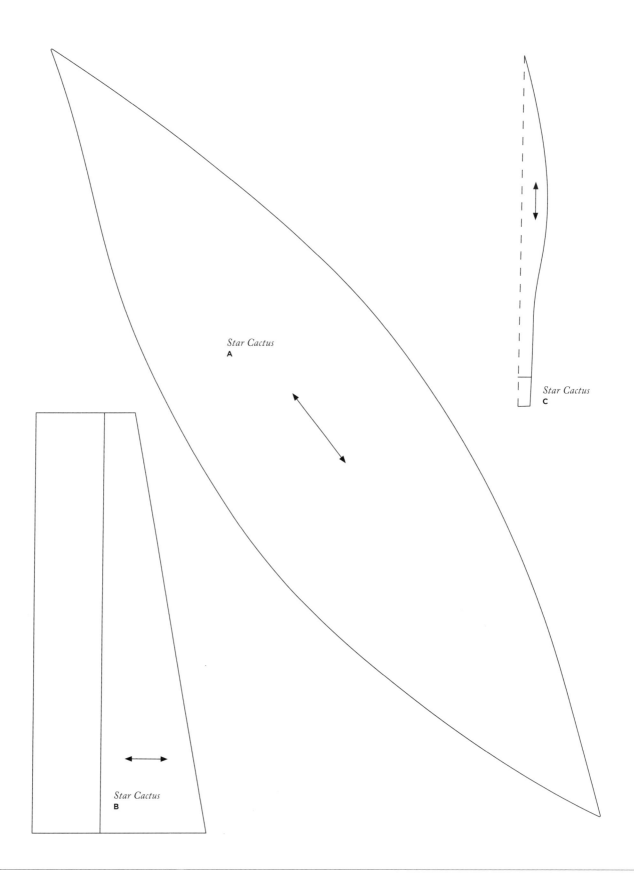

Star Cactus
A

Star Cactus
C

Star Cactus
B

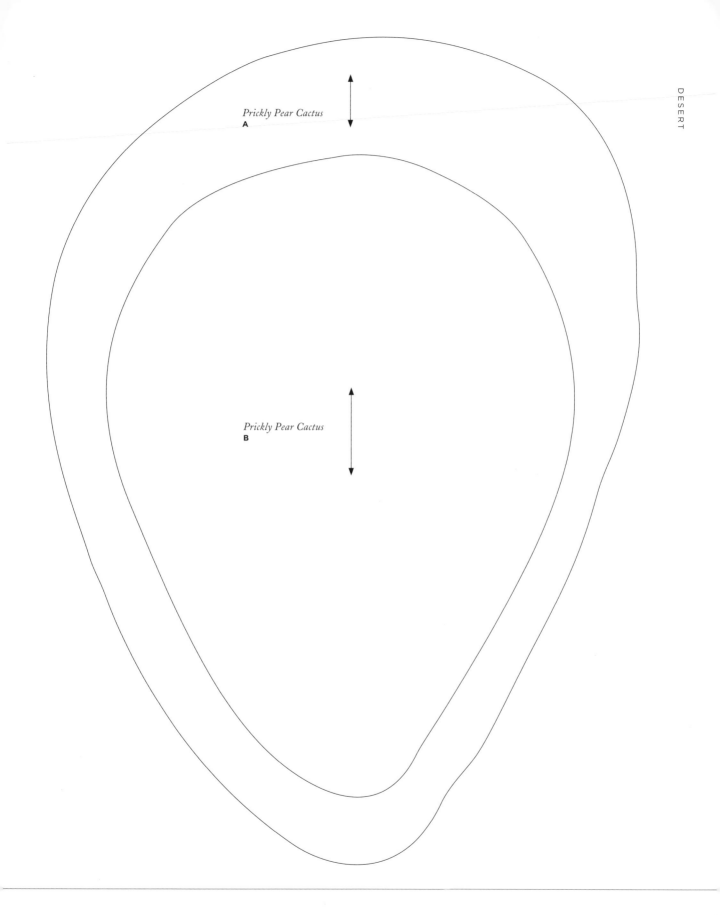

Prickly Pear Cactus
A

Prickly Pear Cactus
B

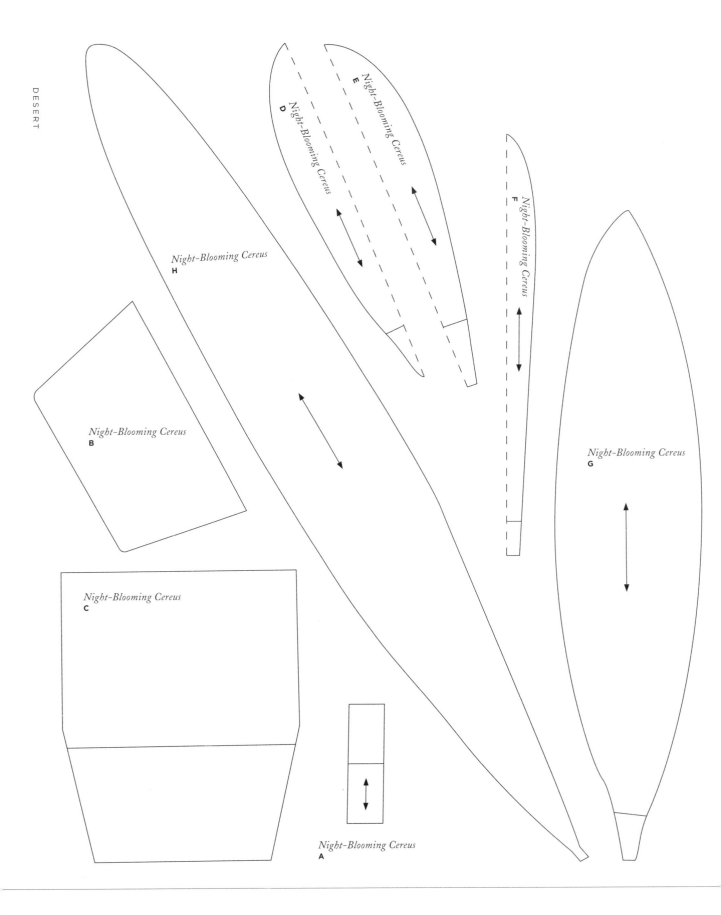

Night-Blooming Cereus
D

Night-Blooming Cereus
E

Night-Blooming Cereus
F

Night-Blooming Cereus
H

Night-Blooming Cereus
B

Night-Blooming Cereus
G

Night-Blooming Cereus
C

Night-Blooming Cereus
A

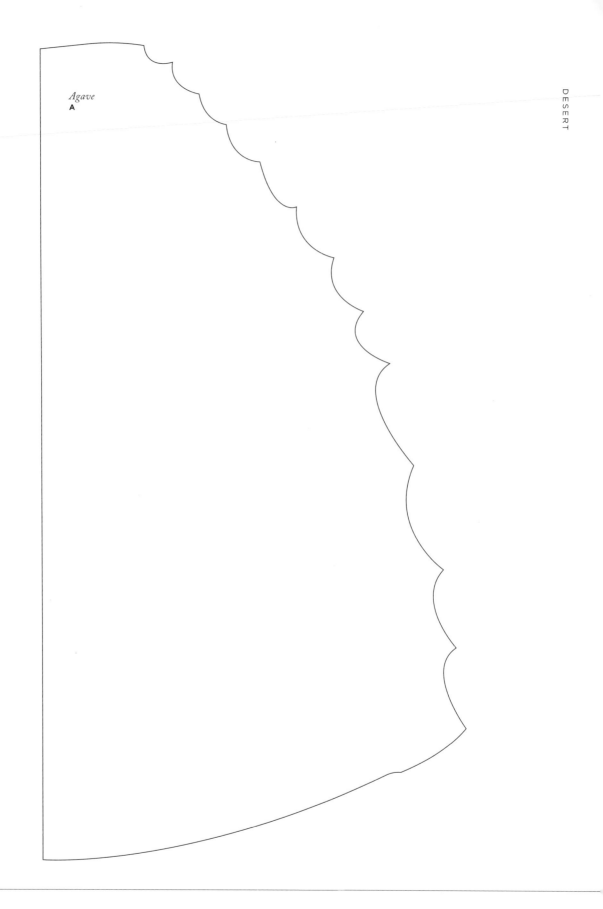

Agave
A

Agave
B

Agave
C

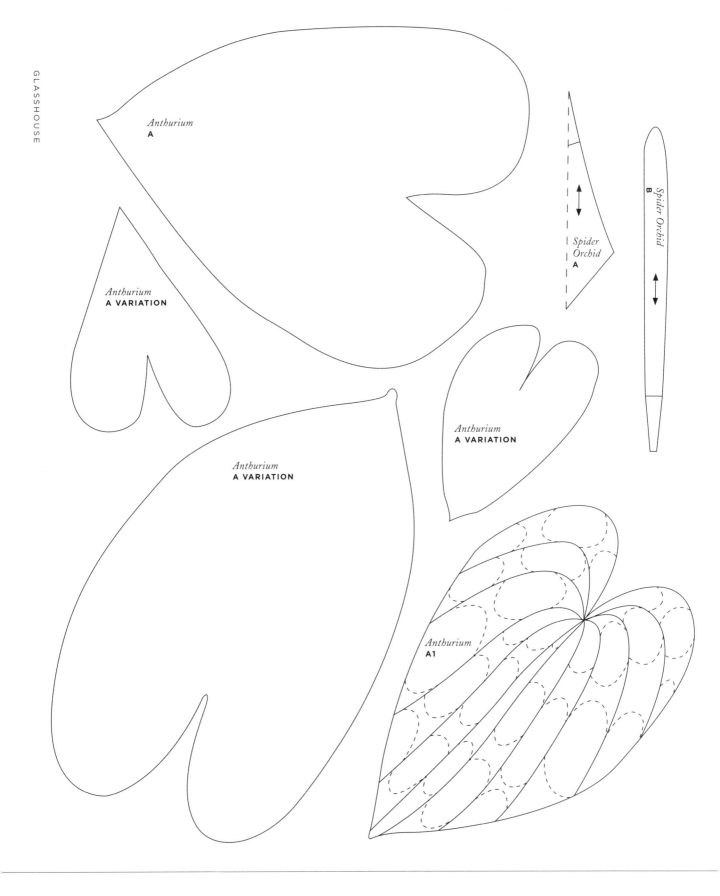

Anthurium
A

Anthurium
A VARIATION

Anthurium
A VARIATION

Anthurium
A VARIATION

Anthurium
A1

Spider Orchid
A

Spider Orchid
B

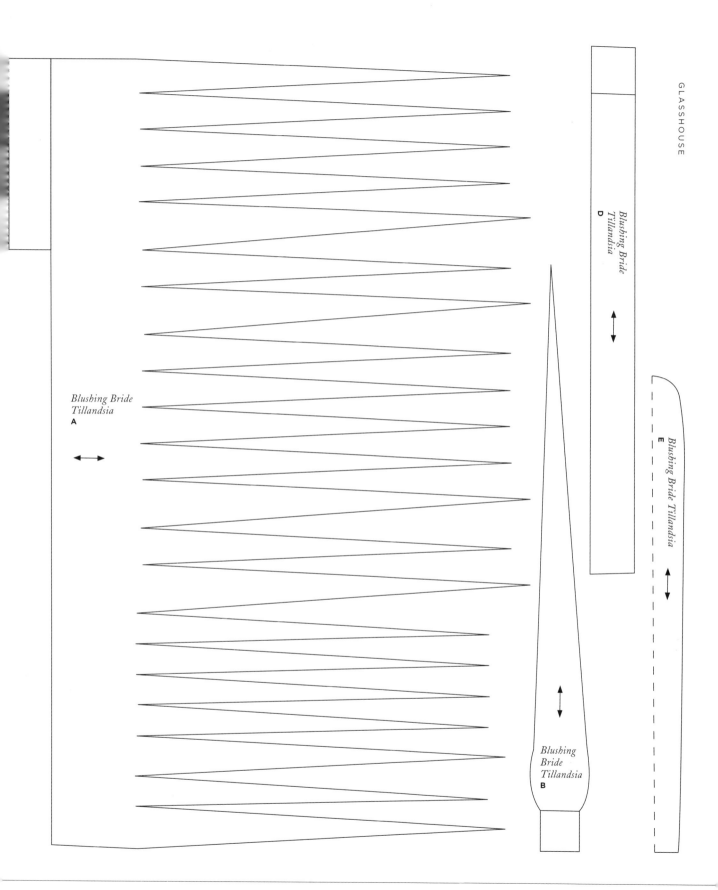

Blushing Bride
Tillandsia
A

Blushing Bride
Tillandsia
B

Blushing Bride
Tillandsia
D

Blushing Bride Tillandsia
E

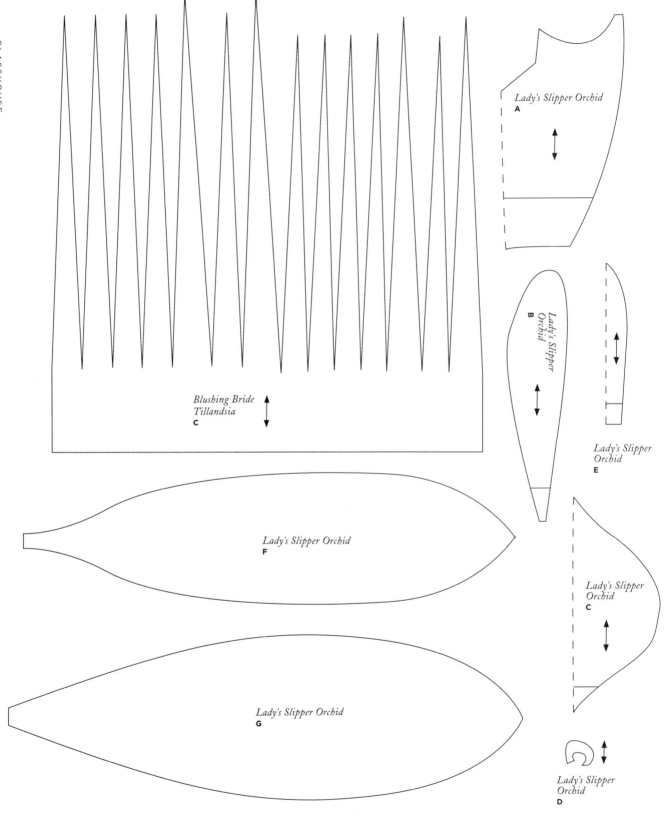

Lady's Slipper Orchid
A

Lady's Slipper Orchid
B

Lady's Slipper Orchid
E

Blushing Bride Tillandsia
C

Lady's Slipper Orchid
F

Lady's Slipper Orchid
C

Lady's Slipper Orchid
G

Lady's Slipper Orchid
D

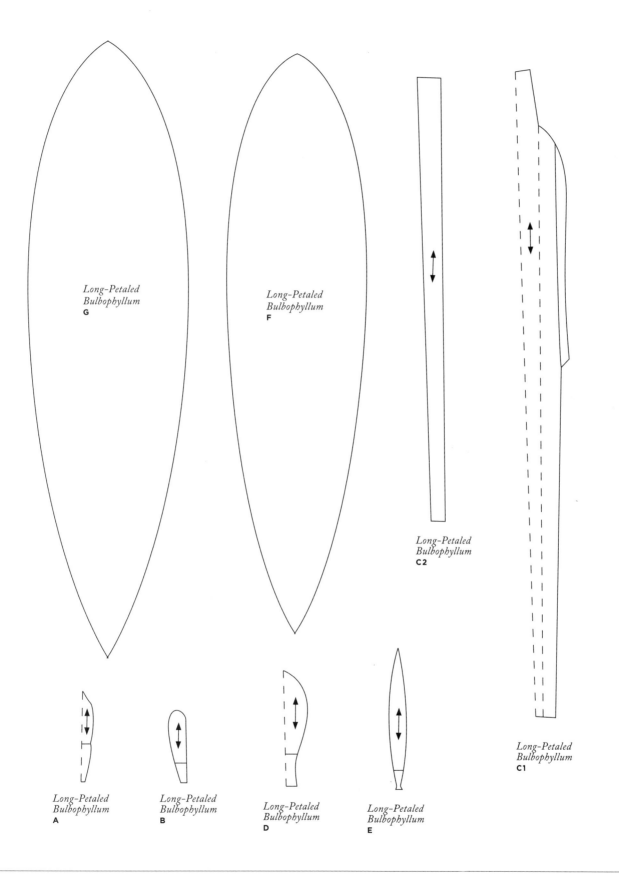

Long-Petaled Bulbophyllum
G

Long-Petaled Bulbophyllum
F

Long-Petaled Bulbophyllum
C2

Long-Petaled Bulbophyllum
C1

Long-Petaled Bulbophyllum
A

Long-Petaled Bulbophyllum
B

Long-Petaled Bulbophyllum
D

Long-Petaled Bulbophyllum
E

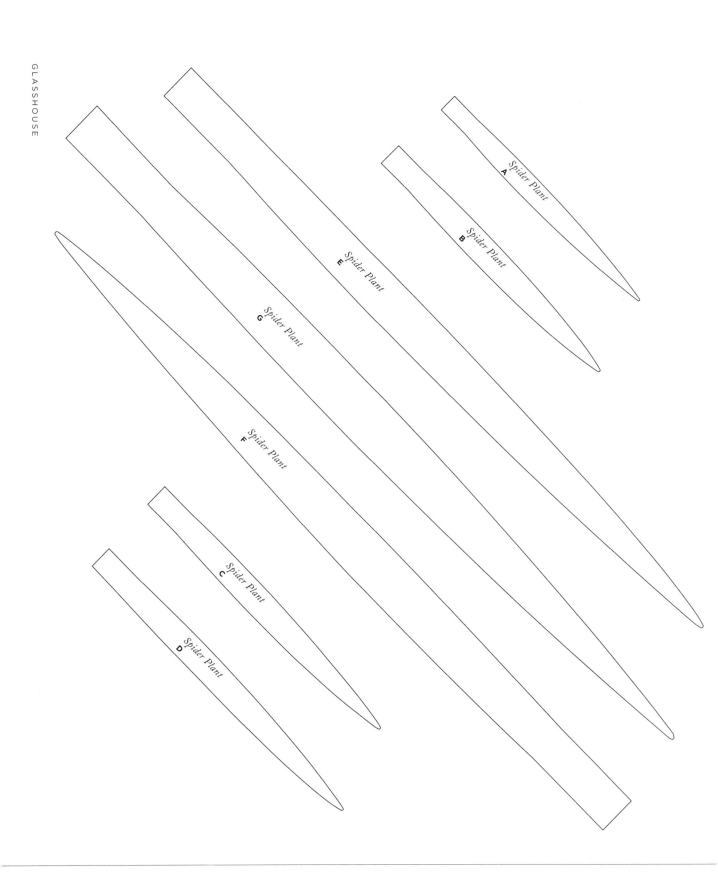

Spider Plant A

Spider Plant B

Spider Plant E

Spider Plant G

Spider Plant F

Spider Plant C

Spider Plant D

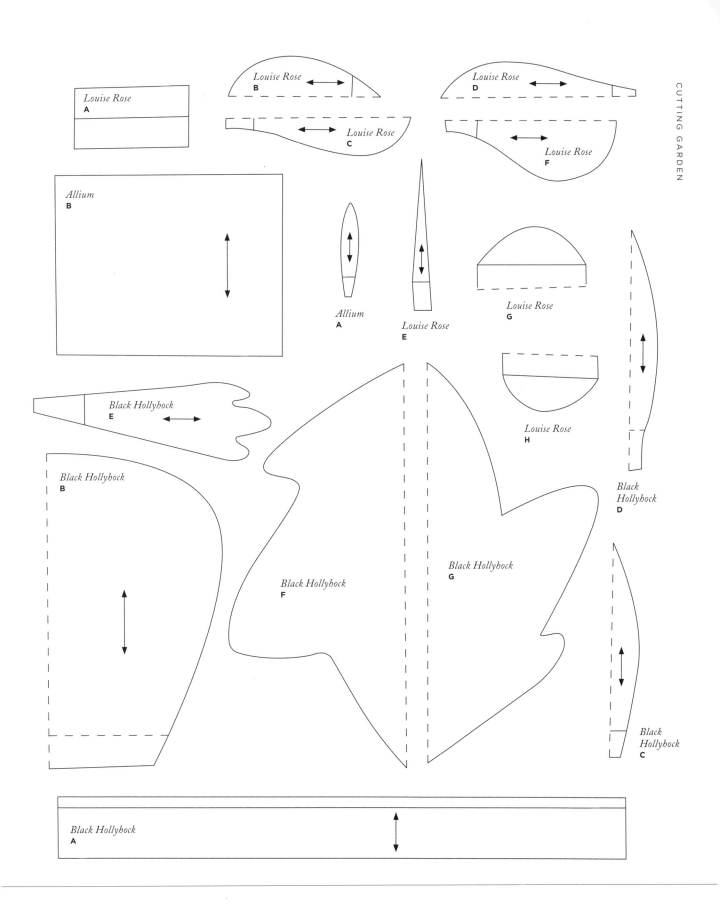

Louise Rose
A

Louise Rose
B

Louise Rose
C

Louise Rose
D

Louise Rose
F

Allium
B

Allium
A

Louise Rose
E

Louise Rose
G

Louise Rose
H

Black Hollyhock
E

Black Hollyhock
B

Black Hollyhock
F

Black Hollyhock
G

Black Hollyhock
D

Black Hollyhock
C

Black Hollyhock
A

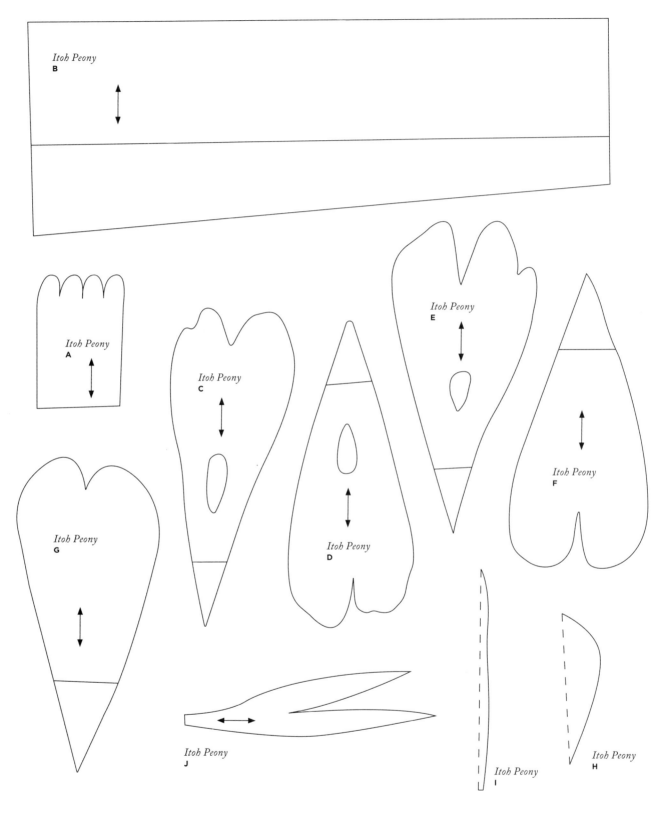

Itoh Peony
B

Itoh Peony
A

Itoh Peony
C

Itoh Peony
E

Itoh Peony
F

Itoh Peony
D

Itoh Peony
G

Itoh Peony
J

Itoh Peony
I

Itoh Peony
H

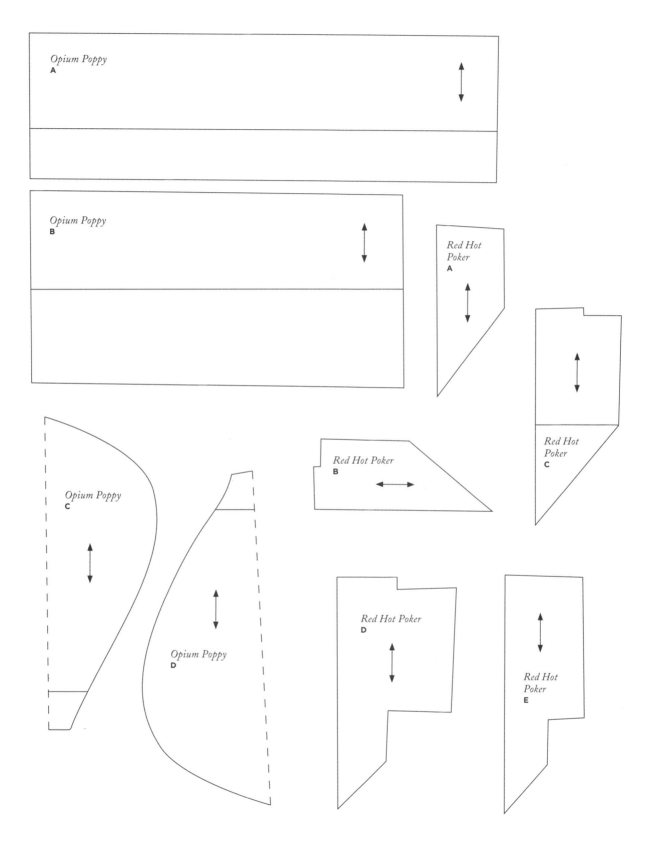

Opium Poppy
A

Opium Poppy
B

Red Hot
Poker
A

Red Hot
Poker
C

Red Hot Poker
B

Opium Poppy
C

Opium Poppy
D

Red Hot Poker
D

Red Hot
Poker
E

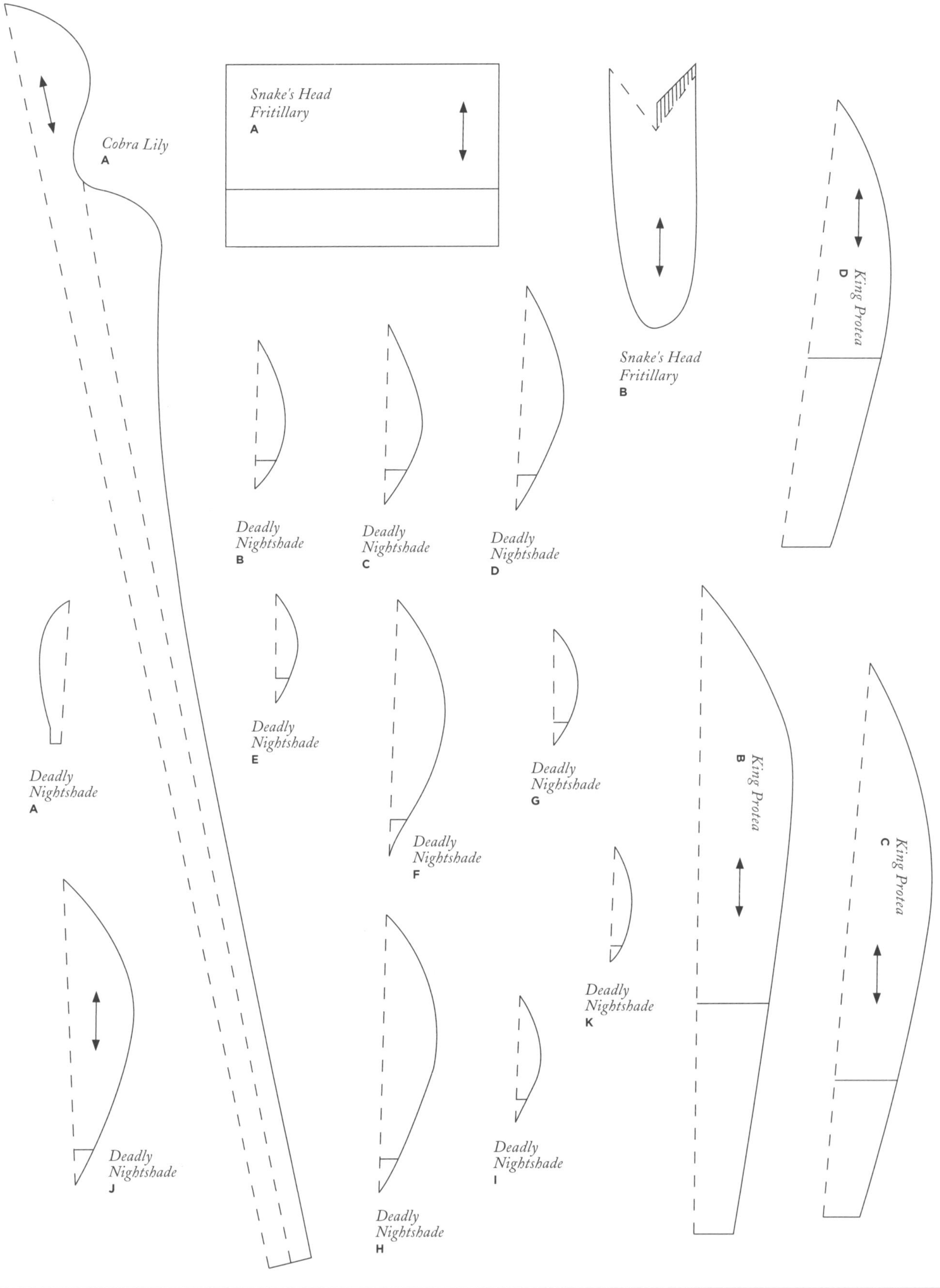

Cobra Lily
A

Snake's Head
Fritillary
A

Snake's Head
Fritillary
B

King Protea
D

*Deadly
Nightshade*
B

*Deadly
Nightshade*
C

*Deadly
Nightshade*
D

*Deadly
Nightshade*
A

*Deadly
Nightshade*
E

*Deadly
Nightshade*
G

King Protea
B

King Protea
C

*Deadly
Nightshade*
F

*Deadly
Nightshade*
K

*Deadly
Nightshade*
J

*Deadly
Nightshade*
I

*Deadly
Nightshade*
H

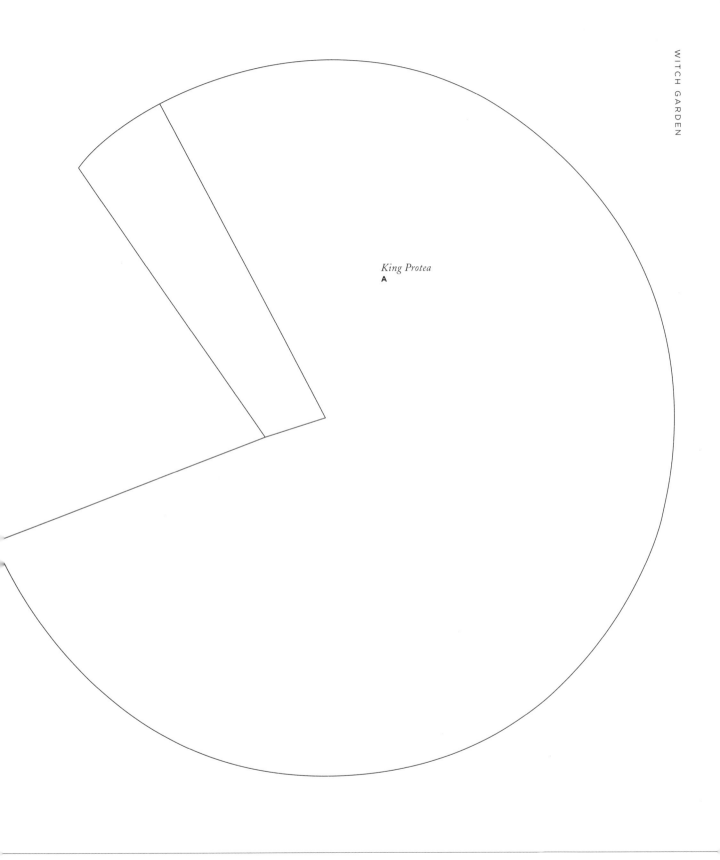

King Protea
A

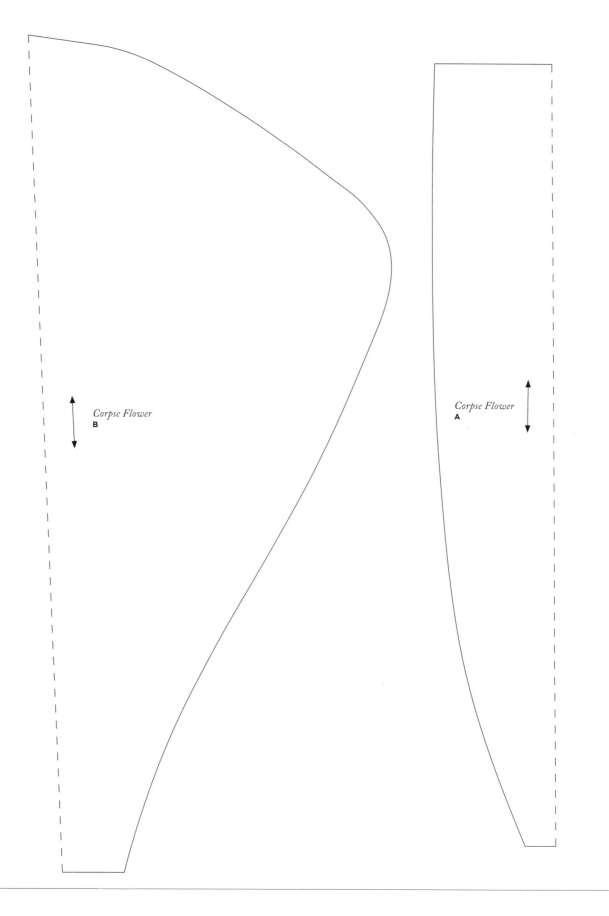

Corpse Flower
B

Corpse Flower
A